THE
TEN COMMANDMENTS
OF
POLITICAL OFFICE

THE
TEN COMMANDMENTS
OF
POLITICAL OFFICE

Naomi Silverthorn

BLUE PLANET
publications
Providing the power of knowledge for a better world.

BLUE PLANET PUBLICATIONS

Blue Planet Publications
PMB 333, 1811 North Dixie Ave., Ste.104,
Elizabethtown, KY 42701

Blue Planet Publications is a division of TVD Consulting

ISBN 10: 0-965741540
ISBN 13: 978-0-9657415-4-5

Published and Printed in the United States of America.

To all of you, and to all of Life.

Life is both a gift and an imperative to make choices.
May we live with a passion for life,
with a love for one another, and may we
choose to govern our government, **now**.

CONTENTS

PART I:
The Ten Commandments of Political Office

PART II:
The Lost Scrolls of American Virtue

PART III:
The Freedom Documents

PART IV:
Participate Relentlessly

ACKNOWLEDGMENTS

Many people touch our lives in meaningful ways and while it's impossible to acknowledge everyone, there are those with whom my soul is entwined in the shared mission of making this world a better place to be.

Bob, the love of my life, has labored with me to birth this book into form. He has an astonishing intellect and uses his gift to share the light of reason and knowledge with many others who seek greater understanding. There is no one more dedicated to the pursuit of truth. His courage, strength, and powerful nurturance of human dignity and liberty is a great example of how to be a progressive human being.

I express my love and gratitude to Glenn, Sandy, and Rocky for their incredible talents, for their support and affection, for their lives of goodness and their love of this nation as stalwart descendants of the American Revolution. They are embodiments of common Americans who are great Americans: intelligent, talented, aware, hard-working, honest, contributing people who consistently serve others quietly, with clear convictions and genuine hearts.

Finally, I wish to acknowledge the beautiful lives of Clem and Dotty, Wendell, Aunt Mary, Uncle Paul, B.L., E.M., and E.P. With thanks and love to them all, for their countless contributions and inspirations through the years.

"To sin by silence when they should protest makes cowards of men."

— Abraham Lincoln

INTRODUCTION

People have asked me why I originally wrote this book. What you are about to read arose from my love of this nation and my compassion for the human condition: there is so much unnecessary suffering in this country caused by a governmental system intractable in its failures to heed the interest of citizens and to govern justly.

The style of this book began as a literary experiment. Because parable and satire transcend words and communicate complicated concepts symbolically, I chose to frame in a language that harkens back to patriots and to the powerful metaphor of scriptural text. Scriptural writers wrote some of the most powerful prose in history and I must acknowledge them for the snippets they provided, as well as acknowledge a little book I recall from many years ago, "The Sayings of Mrs. Solomon" by Helen Rowland. I found it humorous at the time and my recollection of the style was a model for some parts of this book. So if this unusual writing appeals to you, it should not be attributed to my exclusive originality.

People generally assume this book has religious motivations and therefore it's appropriate to inform that this material is not religious in its intention nor philosophy, but is merely a resurrection of ancient wisdom and common sense. There must be no doubt that I ascribe to the founding principles of this free nation separating church and state, so designed because our forebears had suffered crushing oppression by the psychotic, dark child that is ever conceived through a wrongful marriage of religion and politics.

I address this issue at the beginning because this is a book about reclaiming our government through the joining of human hearts, minds, and focused actions. As it stands right now, religious fervor is a fundamental contributor to grave national and world problems, with many of its philosophies allowing no room for solutions or progress.

Of course, there exist many religious, patriotic Americans who try to hold the ground of Liberty. I offer my respect while humbly inviting them to an expanded thought, appealing to their primordial hearts for an awakening of natural human affection and the discernment of reason.

The phrase "God and Country" is a cliché that calls to mind a plethora of other clichés that we generally don't question. Most everyone nods because it sounds good. Unfortunately, we wind up making associations from such a phrase that are neither good nor in the best interests of our democratic republic, where religious freedom is a founding principle. Many

Americans go so far to assert that this is a Christian country, which would mean we have a Church of State, which we do not...even though there are certainly moneyed forces at work to make it so. Historically, politics and religion have worked together to oppress populations and to oppose personal freedom, even so, we have not learned from the many repeating cycles of history.

There is clear evidence, through very troubling follies in recent years, that religious followers are mercilessly used to promote political agendas that give lip service to America while shamelessly gutting its democratic principles behind the scene. Once again, this shows that when freedom is surrendered in one way, it dissolves slowly in other ways, leading to the people being subject by their own consent.

It never fails that religion, being wholly authoritarian of itself, is driven to move its agenda onto the stage of the secular in order to dominate it with sectarian dogma. Far more often than not, religious dogma blinds its adherents to the broader reality of inalienable human rights, absolutely intrinsic to the true freedoms which are not governed by imperatives that arise from religious convictions. When we embrace our beliefs to the extent that we assert that they are the only true blueprint for the human journey and we use our efforts to that end, we are electing to be blinded to the both the freewill of another human being and the

xiii

freedom that is the birthright of all...regardless of whatever iteration of a god and its ideologies they do or do not worship.

When we do this, we are not the redeemers we believe ourselves to be—we are the oppressors.

There is a reason why religious coalitions **have not** and **will not** be able to redeem this nation regardless of their fervor. Although it's a simple matter to understand, the reason escapes those who would most benefit from its realization. At its core, organized religion is a fiercely traditional, human, and *politicized* structure, rooted in things as they once were...and in its very own status quo.

What it will take to save this nation will not be realized in a divided mindset that seeks to uphold one status quo while attempting to tear another one down. Likewise, it is inconceivable to claim freedom or to defend it while at the same time one is conditional about who can have freedom over what issue, and when one is of the mindset that they are superior to others.

Furthermore, governments are instituted among men and women. They are of the physical realm. A Creator of All That Exists has no need for a puny human government and we are certifiably deluded when we feel compelled to deliver governments to God.

This is not the philosophy of genuine greatness that is now needed to align this nation to its destiny. To correct the errors of past and present, the hearts of the American people must emanate an honest commitment to form a compassionate brotherhood, found in our common humanity. We are called upon to abandon any practice that gives lip service to brotherhood while it justifies a darkened spectrum of deceptive divisions. Whether it be hypocritical self-righteous judgments, war and destruction, rage and anarchy, or smug ambivalence in the name of God—a way of taking the easy way out— that which separates us is the real Enemy.

It is long past time that Americans got in touch with the deepest goodness in their own hearts, for it will tell them that respect for Divinity is not about homogenizing the differences in people, it is about **love**. We are at that epic pivotal point in history when the hypocrisy we have practiced will have to be acknowledged and rectified. We will do this by becoming empowered individuals, working together as an authentic Force of One, with an impassioned concern for the welfare of the many.

This book is at variance with the typical, pitiful deference to political power because there is an imperative to make matters right in this nation through restoration of power to the people. This is the way it was meant to be: a government responsive to the needs of the governed through political representation, meaning, politicians and the government agencies must

stand for and **act in the expressed interests of** American citizens, while holding fast to the Constitution.

Our form of government is not a democracy, but a democratic republic, which is based on the rule of law, representative of all the nation's citizens. This is to be distinguished from a democracy, which is based on the rule of the majority and which over time, opens the way for persecution of the few and a bully rule by whatever powerful consensus holds sway at the moment. We may be reminded that this is a nation of equal rights for everyone, not just those we presume to like or agree with, or those with whom we have a tribal allegiance.

All together, it is **entirely appropriate** for the people to hand up their demands to elected officials. The Ten Commandments of Political Office is intended as a **personal letter for Americans to send to each person who represents them in government,** from city council to the White House, for their voices to be heard and to let each representative know that the people are their bosses—and they are expected to hold to a simple list of 10 reasonable mandates to assure the survival of our democratic republic.

Most politicians are lawyers who write entangled legislation that thwarts sensible interpretation, but this bullet-point list of clear and simple truths allows citizens to cut through the political hyperbole that serves to shield officials and to deflect accountability away from them—the standard maneuver by those in power who govern, but do not lead. This clear-cut, commandment style language leaves no room for political officials to wriggle out of the People's Law.

As I wrote this material, I was not acting without precedent. The founding fathers and mothers of our country had risked everything to enforce their demands against a corrupt and degenerate government which had subjugated and persecuted them. I also held a vision of Martin Luther nailing his demands to the Church door at the risk of his own life, representing the power of people to evolve their condition within the constraints of their understanding. And though I never once saw myself on equal terms with those brave people, I had been awakened to a disturbing realization about America. Our country was, and is, at peril from the same dark, oppressive forces of the past, and it is now time to call forth courageous men and women to stand up for human liberty and freedom.

So, today, July 22, 2009, I release this mandate into the hands of my greater American family. Let no one assume it is easy to let fly the words of our collective pain, but it must be done. As the Obama Administration has taken office the nation has slid down a slippery slope, a bi-partisan creation of previous administrations who set the current conditions in motion: from Clinton, to Bush, to Bush... and today, we see that many current Administration appointees were sycophants connected to previous cabals that have crafted the situation as it now stands.

Yet again, this proves that in politics, the more things change "the more they stay the same." At all times, let us strenuously evaluate the actions of government as to whether it serves Constitutional principles and the people of this nation, or whether elite groups and factions continue to manipulate the process at the expense of all that America stands for. Let us undertake immediate, unrelenting initiative should the new administration prove to be a frightful descendant of the old, for the status quo is *perniciously embedded* in government.

Americans must demand absolute truth from their politicians and every government agency and demand an immediate return to exacting democratic governance. We must understand the consequences of our past mistakes and hold political power to the People's Law. I join with many other Americans in a heartfelt call to action: if it resonates with you, please tell others about this. Each one of us and all of us together are faced with the decision to make the difference, and to do so without another moment of delay.

May we nail our list to the tree of Liberty.

THE
TEN COMMANDMENTS
OF
POLITICAL OFFICE

"When the people fear their government, there is tyranny; when the government fears the people, there is liberty. "

—**Thomas Jefferson**

Part One

THE
TEN COMMANDMENTS
OF
POLITICAL OFFICE

"Every government degenerates when trusted to the rulers of the people alone. The people themselves are its only safe depositories."

—Thomas Jefferson

PREAMBLE

Our very special country has lost its way, partly because many Americans have become disconnected from the roots of their destined identity and have thus allowed those in power to reshape America's mien, bearings, and conduct. We have strayed sufficiently at this point that a great many people are feeling alarmed, asking themselves and each other, "What has happened to this country?!"

While national problems are immense on practically every level of government and society, it's essential to tackle simple but significant matters first, moving forward from there. Often, the most obvious matters are overlooked and so let us begin our journey to wellness by remembering that *this* nation is *not* "The Homeland." Let us cast aside that surreptitiously imposed and infamous designation, leaving it buried forever in the ruins of a Nazi regime, never to resurrect. Its menacing connotation reveals a sinister trend that is far from patriotic and it should not be tolerated as a part of our democratic vernacular.

No matter what ideas are put forward to shape public opinion, what actions are taken to realign

1

the nation, or how many words are used perversely, it is not unpatriotic to resist false patriotism.

Patriotism is not what we are led to believe in these Orwellian times: compliance with the status quo, silence in the face of usurpations, submission to the stripping away of Constitutional protections. Patriotism means what it has always meant: the love and defense of one's country. In no way should it mean we embrace executive orders dictated by a term in office, a nation of political appointees with broad powers that usurp the political process, a nation of police powers or assorted "czars," or that just about anything and everything government decides to do has to be okay with us. Patriotism means that we stand up for this Constitutional, representative nation of liberty and justice for all.

Through genuine patriotism we will redeem our nation from its careening course because we will stop being silent and compliant and hopelessly passive. We will participate relentlessly to govern our government.

To trouble ourselves with the workings of government is the price of living in a free society and few humans in the history of nations have had the privilege of doing so. The founders of The United States of America bequeathed to this world a great experiment and established an enlightened social system of self-governance. Their model of freedom can only flourish when a society is absent from the rule of the one or of the elite few, when people are enabled to set their own agendas, arrange their own economy, ponder the mysteries of life according to their own conscience, provide for justice and equality, and govern the government they install to serve them.

As the rule of law, our Constitution and the Bill of Rights were established to protect this nation against a potential—indeed, probable—deconstruction of its founding principles. Our founders, wise in the way of spiritual forces and the seduction of power as it plays out in the human ego, knew that dark-sided tyranny never sleeps, that it can seduce those who have been granted power by trust, and that it would inevitably seek a stronghold over the American people.

The exclamations in this material are rigorously expressed by people in private, but under an Orwellian political correctness they are seldom made public. A great many people choose to keep quiet for fear of being labeled extreme. Many others are conditioned to believe that intelligent moderation is equivalent to silence and compliance.

While silence and compliance work very well in other forms of government, *these behaviors do not sustain a democratic republic.*

3

Americans have reason to harbor the deepest concerns about this country's present course and thus, our future. Whether the inept response to a warning about a pending terrorist attack that would eventually be known as 9-11, inconsequential excuses for an invasion of Iraq, assorted Constitutional affronts, a collapsed economy, globalist trends, indictments on politicians...there are many indicators that America is no longer the land of our fathers. Whatever we have thus uncovered, these are a mere glancing blow at the political Goliath that wounds our national body, with intention and without remorse.

Americans must become educated about what every political hack takes to be a fact: politics is about what's in it for the politically powerful, not about the American people or the good of the nation. Far too many Americans, for far too long, have been prone to sit still and hope that a hero archetype, the proverbial wise father, will provide for them or save them. And while hope is nurtured in the collective mind as a worthwhile virtue, hope can also be an expectation a person engenders when he feels no power over a situation and thus, waits for beneficent circumstances to occur. In Banana Republics and Communist countries, hope is *all* that people have. The politically powerless comply with their regimes and silently hope for things to get better.

4

Let us realize, right here and right now, that
while hope inspired this great democracy, hope is
not sufficient to keep it. Consistent, relentless action
by an informed population is required...and
nothing less.

The new Administration faces unprecedented
challenges in practically every venue of
governance, including the imperative to reverse
Constitutional infractions perpetrated by the Bush/
Cheney years and restore our adherence to
Constitutional law. Americans must demand that
changes promised include complete accountability
of their entire government across-the-board,
including a complete cessation of all infringement
on personal liberties and comprehensive
accountability for the immoral, scandalous
activities of the financial markets and the
inexcusable collapse of the American economy.

To reestablish justice in this nation citizens must
stand together. Despite a present transitory hope,
there still exists shallow, artificial divisions related
to political parties, religious preferences, race,
economic status, education, age, and so on. We are
called upon to heal the trivialities that separate us
in a whole new way because we are all in this
together, as a national family. We need to realize
that the unity of the people is most dreaded by
tyrants. What cabal can withstand the force of

millions, bonded together in the common devotion to their own good?

A free society remains free because it fosters tolerance among its people and fairness in its government. If this nation is to survive, Americans will find the abuses of government that oppress even one person in this nation subject to their swift response. We will change from being inhibited and afraid, to empowered beings of courageous character with a just interest in the welfare of others. We will ensure that a government designed to serve the people does *only* and *exactly* what it was installed by the people to do.

We will, from our own spiritual understanding, inspire by example. We will be what we preach. And the world, because it is made up of divine souls the same as us, will respond.

The truth is, we have gotten the government we have allowed. Freedom is so precious yet our nation will go the way of its people. Some will not surrender their selfish interests nor will they care until it is too late.

When the age of hope and achievement passes, history has shown that a Dark Age ensues, lasting for ages and for generations. Is this what you want? Will you be imprisoned in a false freedom by working several jobs into your old age? Will you allow yourself to be measured by bureaucracy as a mere consumer? Are you a managed human resource — or are you a sentient, free being?

We must not worry what others may think of us if we go against the grain of popular opinion. The battle to develop this nation was a non-conformist choice by visionaries who had experienced oppression, injustice, and elitism until their very souls could bear no more.

Do you believe that the object of all good government is self-government, and that a government of the People, by the People and for the People is a shining standard to an endangered world? Would you choose to live less than this? Will you cave in to the propaganda of fear and sell your soul because you are so saturated with complexity that you can no longer find the simple truth that you are born free?

Pain avoidance is what the bureaucrats have counted on. There is no such thing as no pain and there is no escape. We do not need to be falsely protected. We must embrace the risk of living and there is no freedom without inherent dangers. A totally protected society is a fascist society.

Truth has a way of speaking to the human heart. May an increasing number of Americans open their hearts to the realization of our condition, however much courage that requires. As generations before, let us now lock arms and mutually pledge that we will save this nation—and thus ourselves—by the way that we live our lives, by whatever fortune we may possess, and by our sacred honor.

"**B**ut what do we mean by the American Revolution? Do we mean the American war? The Revolution was effected before the war commenced. The Revolution was in the minds and hearts of the people... This radical change in the principles, opinions, sentiments, and affections of the people was the real American Revolution."

—John Adams

THE
TEN COMMANDMENTS
OF
POLITICAL OFFICE

scribed upon the reverse side of foreclosure notices; sorely etched upon parchment of American sheepskins and handed up to those in high places; for behold, from North, South, East and West, the People **roareth**, saying:

ONE.

Thou Shalt Have No Special Interests Before Us.

Yea, thou shalt not bow down to them nor serve them, lest the land become corrupt.

Thou shalt honor the People that electeth thee, all thy days in office. Hear the words of our mouths and obey them.

Yea, thou shalt not forsake the People for three years and then embrace them again

11

on election year with strategized artifice.
For behold, in this cunning thou art like
unto the prodigal wife who returneth unto
her husband after many years, saying, "Lo,
I am an attentive and devoted wife, thou
art one with mine own loins and it shall be
like we hath not been apart."

And it shall come to pass that the cunning of
this woman shall be revealed unto her
husband and he shall drive her out. Yea,
her lies are known because of her works.
Yea, she hath betrayed his trust—and from
this, there is no deliverance.

TWO.

Thou Shalt Preserve, Protect, & Defend the Constitution of The United States of America.

Thou shalt not usurp the Constitution for any
cause or under any circumstance; **in**

12

principal or in fact. Thou shalt not whittle away its protections , nor permit any office or branch or person to commit this crime of high treason.

Thou shalt not shift untoward powers over this Nation to political appointees, nor permit the Executive Branch to seize untoward powers by order or by subterfuge. Yea, this is a government of democratic representation; yea, all powers of unrighteous rule that hath been funneled to the Executive Branch and its appointees shall be toppled with rigor, **straightaway**.

Thou shalt not engender military, security, or police forces to set themselves against this People. Yea, our first president hath said that overgrown military establishments are inauspicious to liberty. Yea, *civil unrest means thou hast not done thy job.*

Thou shalt be vigilant in the protection of Liberty; yea, She is most pure and comely, desired and beloved above all else by free beings in all of existence; yea, and the shadows of power despise her, to bind her with great chains unto death.

Thou hast been entrusted to preserve, protect, and defend the Constitution and he who trespasses against it shall have no forgiveness in this political dispensation, nor will any come again. Yea, the roots of his influence shall be plucked from polluted ground, and he shall be cast into political **fire.**

THREE.

Thou Shalt Not Worship the Graven Image of Power.

Thou shalt not concentrate power into the hands of the few, or of the one.

Thou shalt not make laws under cover of night. Neither shalt thou govern by fear, nor be governed by fear. Thou shalt not yield to panic legislation nor weaken under threat, nor coercion, nor temptation of banishment, neither by the powers above thee, nor by extortion nor by bribe.

For what doth it profit a politician if he gaineth the world and loseth his Soul?

Thou shalt not devise laws written in tongues, weaving and twining many

14

words that only the merchants of law do profit there from.

Yea, thy words shall be small and plain as unto a babe, and few, as unto a humbled husband before his brawling wife.

Lo! The People need no lawmakers who delight in the splitting of hairs and who hath no sense for the breaking burdens they heap. Yea, a true leader knoweth the object of all good government is self government; yea, he maketh few laws and keepeth them all.

Thou shalt not make unto the common man a criminal according to sundry and fanatic suspicions; neither shalt thou cultivate citizens to suspect one another, neither shalt thou comb through a citizen's privacy like a tweezer that seeketh the lice. In this, ye do strain at a gnat and swallow a camel; yea, Justice is toppled to ruin.

Thou shalt not engage in any warfare nor empower foreign armies without the consensus of the People; yea, and thine offering unto them shall be of due diligence and utter truth.

15

Thou shalt not crouch down to hide thy doings and do-nothings; neither thy contributors nor those on the take. Thou shalt not hide the light of disclosure under a bush; nor empower by bargain or bribe, by favor or fraternity, or commit any villainy like unto it.

For it shall come to pass that he who confesses his crimes shall have a just sentence, that he may yet renew his worth—but he that conceals complicities and countenances corruption shall be stricken by political demise, **never to rise again.**

FOUR.

Thou Shalt Not Spend the Money of the People in Vain.

The People will not hold him guiltless that spendeth their money in vain.

Yea, thou shalt not heap thy tables nor oil thy bodies with money earned upon the swain backs of a freeborn People, neither of this generation nor of the generations yet to come.

Verily, O Wastrels, our money is our heartbeats; yea, we hath amassed it with our very lives.

Ye shall not squander our lives.

Thou shalt not spend the people's money to gain influence nor to engage in subterfuge. Thou shalt not spend the People's money on barrels of pork or black budgets. Neither shalt thou fatten the devouring beasts, the crippled bureaucracies that parseth a drop while they inhaleth the oceans. Thou shalt not conceal gluttonous spending within the pages of onerous legislation. Thou shalt not pilfer the People's money with deceitful double-speak; yea, thy trespasses against us hath amassed to the heavens and we are **sorely provoked.**

Thou shalt not burden the People with debt.

Thou shalt not spend the People's money to profit the greed of the rich, nor to profit the banks, nor quasi-government agencies, nor corporations, nor companies, nor other nations, nor foreign armies, nor for the benefit of the few, nor to amass thine own treasury, nor the treasury of thy kith nor kin.

Yea, whatsoever elected official arrangeth a debt shall be first in line to pay it, unto the seed of his own generations that follow. Yea, thou shalt be fiscally responsible or thou shalt rue thine election like unto a day of doom. Yea, for a silo of riches shalt thou be burdened with poverty; yea, thou shalt be branded with shame.

Thou shalt not spend the money of the People in vain.

FIVE.

Remember the Working Day, to Keep it Productive.

Thou shalt earn thy wages or not be paid. Yea, the People knoweth the idleness of thy days; yea, when they are in need of bread ye give them a stone; yea, the good of the Nation never gets done.

Lo, many there be who hoggeth time in office while they doeth not any good work, for the political kingdom is a sluggard's paradise. Yea, thine holidays are multitude and thine absences art grievous. Yea, thy pay raises are without merit and slither into thy pockets under cover of night, without the will of the People. Therefore thou shalt repent **straightaway.**

For verily we say unto you, **ye are not too important to labor.** Therefore thou shalt remember the working day, to keep it productive.

SIX.

Thou Shalt Not Kill, Nor Do Anything Like Unto It.

Thou shalt not murder the truth, neither cut it asunder, neither smother it with honeyed

19

words nor suffocate it in a sealed jar. Yea, O Cunning Ones, thou shalt not slay the truth by thy method of presentation.

Thou shalt not kill the civilians of any nation. Thou shalt not assassinate nor torture any person, nor destroy land nor kill Liberty, nor starve Justice nor slay Hope, in this nation or any nation on the face of the sanctified Earth. Thou shalt not work corruption in the hallowed name of the United States of America, nor represent thy crimes as done in the name of its People.

Thou shalt not kill the economy.

Thou shalt not starve the People's potential; yea, thou shalt not strip the nation's treasures as the locusts devour the wheat.

Thou shalt not kill the taxpayer, for he layeth the golden egg.

Lo, he who taxeth the People without representation and who taxeth them to ruin shall be declared an enemy of the Republic, straightaway. Lo, remember this, lest the People drag thee to another riotous Party of Tea.

Yea, to taxeth the camel, the hoof, the straw,
the stream, the tent, the table, the babe,
the jug, the pipe, the bread, the wine, the
vineyard, the fruit, the bones, the pyre,
the fire, the plough, the path, the sky, the
sun, the moon and stars is to make thyself
as unto Pharaoh and to make the People
as slaves of an utterly corrupted kingdom.
Yea, in these crimes hath thou slain Hope
and pierced the heart of Liberty.

Yea, he who destroys the promise of our lives
shall not go out in glory, but shall go
down in infamy. He shall be cast out
naked and shall be made **utterly barren
of honor.**

SEVEN.

Thou Shalt Not Commit Adulterous Alliances.

Yea, thou shalt not commit fornication with
corporations, nor incest with insiders, nor
lust after war nor the profits of war, nor
lay thyself down with lobbyists, money

21

changers, traders, with any corruptor of the Republic, foreign or domestic.

Yea, O Lofty Ones, thou shalt vow upon the Altar of Liberty to never be seduced. For behold, know thou that what can be corrupted, will be corrupted.

Be ye therefore clean.

Thou shalt not compromise the position of thine office, nor the supremacy of the Constitution, nor the good of the People for thou art wedded unto us. Thou shalt not betray the People's trust; neither shalt thou partake of secret samplings upon a bed of shame.

For behold, thine actions shall be proclaimed from the rooftops and thy blindness shall be made known, **lest thou leadest thy nation into a ditch.**

EIGHT.

Thou Shalt Not Steal.

Yea, thou shalt not steal from a person or from a company, from a bank or from a pension fund, from an expense account, from the federal budget, or from a public purse. Thou shalt not steal from the poor to give unto the rich, **nor do anything like unto it**.

Thou shalt not steal away the Constitutional rights of this People as thieves that come in the night. Neither shalt thou steal their land nor their possessions to make greater the strength of the government over the People.

Thou shalt be watchful about the borders of this Nation. For behold, we hath been known by foreign lands as a great and glittering table on a hill, heaped upon with wheat and set about with lilies, and many there be that come to us for plenty.

And while the People are filled with charity and virtue toward those who suffer, thou hast slept at the Gate and the table is stripped; lo, the nation is like unto a woman whose womb has borne thirty of her kind and like unto a husband who hath too many babes to feed. Behold, they faint and perish, all.

Yea, the Land of Promise is gone brittle and lean, like a twig in the snow; yea, our inheritance is bartered as interest on debts.

Yea, the body cannot endure the wantonness ye engender. Ye shall not foster wantonness. Thou shalt protect this Nation's sovereignty with all thy heart, mind, might and strength. Yea, the parent of a greater freedom must be allowed to prosper, that goodly generations among all men may yet come to pass.

Thou shalt not sell, or lease, or create union with, or barter American soil to foreign interests, nor let the public land to private interests; for verily, ye cannot take or trade or sell or lease what ye do not own.

Behold, ye are servants of this household.

Thou shalt not take this nation unto thyself.

Yea, thou shalt not steal in principle or in fact. Yea, he that stealeth shall be cast to the lions as a boulder is heaved from a cliff and he shall topple to his **utter political destruction.**

24

NINE.

Thou Shalt Not Slander Thine Adversary.

Yea, thou shalt not falsely accuse any person or any nation.

Thou shalt not be as the hypocrites who defame, who appear holy while they stinketh with rot.

Thou shalt not blame thy neighbor for thine own failings.

Thou shalt have dignity toward him that taketh a different view. Thou shalt reserve thine accusations to be offered in formal charges of misconduct and then thy grievance shall be made righteous or **thou shalt be made ashamed.**

TEN.

Thou Shalt Not Covet.

Thou shalt not covet a rich man's houses, nor
his yachts, nor his Swiss bank accounts,
nor his power; yea, thou shalt not covet
anything outside thy lawfully appointed
gain, **lest the land become corrupt.**

*For up from the darkened Valley of
Thunder ascendeth the Voice of a unified and
rageful People, saying:*

Whosoever keepeth these sayings shall
have honor in the land, and not be cast out.
Yea, such a one shall be revered; yea, he shall
be esteemed beyond the little days of man.

But lo, whosoever forsaketh these sayings;
yea, whosoever corrupteth the land and

chaineth the Republic shall be pulled down from power straightaway. Such shall pass into utter infamy, unto days without end.

For as hath been said in times of old, the humble grass that bendeth with the winds of storm returneth upright afterward, but the mighty oak that bendeth not, falleth hard.

So shall it be unto you.

"It behooves our citizens to be on their guard, to be firm in their principles and full of confidence in themselves. We are able to preserve our self-government if we will but think so."

— Thomas Jefferson

Part Two

THE
LOST SCROLLS
OF
AMERICAN VIRTUE

"All tyranny needs to gain a foothold is for people of good conscience to remain silent."
—Thomas Jefferson

THE
BOOK OF
EXPECTATIONS

O, who can find a virtuous politician? His price
is far above the National Debt, **for he cannot
be bought.**

The hearts of the People safely trust in him; he
doth *not* increase his pay against popular
opinion; he doth *not* make laws under cover
of night, and his bank drafts doth *not* bounce
like sour grapes upon the floor of Congress.

Lo, he will do the People good all the days of his
office. Yea, the virtuous politician seeketh the
voice of the People, while he regardeth
lobbyists with wisdom. Yea, he knoweth their
hidden devices and that their folly is set in
great dignity; yea, he shall not be like unto the
polluted ones who *eateth,* then *wipeth their
mouths* and say: *"I have done nothing illegal."*

Lo! The virtuous politician is one who taketh
short lunches and ordereth not from the most

expensive menu. Yea, if he drooleth over the mandarin-glazed goose, he payeth for it *himself.* Behold, he doth not squander the People's shekels and he glutteth not himself on their labors, for he knoweth that he who is greedy might eventually get caught, but he who *hateth gifts* shall have the blessing of the People.

The virtuous politician affordeth his clothes by an honest income. Yea, he knoweth that if he is influenced by bribes, incentives, or shady financial dealings, the finest threads of gold *will not hide the rottenness of his bones.*

He openeth his mouth, and lo! there is only **truth**. In his tongue is the law of equality and justice; he knoweth that a hypocrite by his mouth destroyeth. Yea, he *careth* about the People and he knoweth that their freedom *slippeth* and *slideth* upon the *oily words* of whitewashed politicians who *profess honesty* while they *practice corruption.*

Behold, when he speecheth to his fellows, he doth not refer to the People as *"they"* ; but instead, he sayeth "we." Yea, he considereth himself not apart from the People for he knoweth he is *a part of* the People! Yea, he knoweth that his election is an enlistment to *service* and he loatheth membership in the Big Boy's Club.

The virtuous politician ariseth early and attendeth to his elected duties; he hath great vision for his country and he *organizeth* his time while he eliminateth wasteful *organization.* Yea, **see how he gets the job done!** He cutteth out armies of staffers and innumerable costly, bureaucratic , time-killing, hair-splitting, ego-inflating meetings that narrow his focus upon the *head of a pin* and keep him out of *critical legislative debate.* Yea, he dealeth with the People's issues and because he hath true intellect and decisive leadership, he aptly arrangeth the pieces of a problem into one great whole. Lo and behold! He chaseth not his tail, but **he beginneth to lead.**

The virtuous politician maketh *sensible laws* and he maketh them with *few words.* He utterly abhorreth a multitude of double-talking. He doth not spend more legislative time debating renovation of the Capitol Hair *Salon* than the Savings and Loan *Scandal;* such a thing is an

33

abomination unto him. Yea, he debateth *not at all* about *wallpaper and doorknobs*, for lo! he is responsible like unto a physician, who, when a dying man cometh to him, he tryeth not to *comb his hair*, but instead, to *save his life*.

Yea, a virtuous politician is to be more admired than a whale that walketh, for he *cureth corruption* and *limiteth his perks*. He putteth the interests of the People before the interests of the Party and he yieldeth not to perverse partisan politics. Yea, he acteth like a *grown man* instead of a *small boy* in a dirt pile that squabbleth over trinkets. Lo and behold! His razor mind cutteth to the heart of popular perceptions; yea, *he maketh timely and sensible decisions*.

He rideth his camel along the *straight* and *narrow* budgetary *line*. He doth not allow the king's soldiers to spend $1,868.15 per chamber pot seat. He smiteth down those who spendeth $100,000 to study the effect of jet noise on pregnant horses and he would rather leap to the *bottom of a shaft*, than to *shaft the People* with ransom-priced elevator flooring that shuttles wayward feet down to *empty* chambers and up to needless *committees*.

Yea, he utterly beheadeth those who pillage the
public purse! He choppeth asunder the many
gangrenous hands that slink within the
shadows of an embellished government to
skim the *sweetened cream* for themselves and
leave the *sour curds* for the People! He raiseth
not taxes, but he allotteth more services
because he is the *right man for the job.* Yea, he
knoweth all the onerous expenditures there
are to hatchet, *and he beginneth to carve.* Lo,
and behold! The virtuous politician returneth
the spoils of a midnight theft; yea, he giveth
himself a pay reduction.

Behold, he knoweth all the many oppressions in
his own nation and he stretcheth outward his
hand. He useth his power to help his own
country; yea, he maketh a righteous nation so
there are no oppressed among the People.

He feareth not the surrender of his position, for
he knoweth that a politician who hoggeth
entrusted time in office is likened unto a
rolling swine that weareth diamonds in its
snout.

Surely, his people shall rise up and call him
blessed, for self-serving power is like the

tinkling of sleet against glass, but a politician that serveth the People shall be praised.

Yea, generations of children shall reap the fruits of his good works. Freedom prevaileth because of his virtue; there is peace, prosperity, and justice upon all the land. Yea, his good works are his reward, and *that is all he wanteth.*

"It behooves every man who values liberty of conscience for himself, to resist invasions of it in the case of others: or their case may, by change of circumstances, become his own."

—Thomas Jefferson

THE
BOOK OF WAILINGS

Many of the People suffer in silence, but lo, many among them howleth out loud, saying: thou politicians, my elected leaders, **why hast thou forsaken me?**

For behold, I have sought thee with much words to the pollsters; I have paraded outside thy gates. Thy watchmen about the country seeth my nakedness, but **thou regardeth me not.**

Yea, the sound of my trouble groweth loud as the roaring of great lions. I cry in the daytime; in the night, my wailing and the sirens of police chariots at war with evildoers rend the darkness.

I am not silent; even so, thou regardeth me not.

For behold, thou art within thy gardens of sweet-smelling lilies and designer perfumes; wheat and barley heap upon thy tables, thy portion is fat and thy meat plenteous; thy perks of gold, silver, and jet rides occupy thy time. Thou taketh my last shekel and though I am likened to a shorn lamb for the slaughter, ye are not satisfied.

Yea, thou squandereth my money and increaseth my taxes. Thy hardened heart is without understanding; yea, thine ears art deaf and thine eyes art blind but thy lizard's tongue flappeth without ceasing.

Yea, ye cry out for sweet wine from sour grapes. Foreign nations trust in thee: thou dost deliver them, dine with them, and gird up their economies. Yea, in a proclamation of triumph thou dost fling away America's farm and factory with a hallowed countenance and a sense of accomplishment.

Yea, **thou art much absent from home.**

Lo, though I butter thy bread and make thee to sit in high places and soar upon the wings of an Eagle, I am to thee but a useless eater, an uncomely aardvark that groveleth in the dust. Yea, I am utterly common, and despised of thee. I am also despised of the foreign ones;

yea, I am laughed to scorn! They shake their heads, saying: "Behold the lazy one who beggeth at the tables of our enterprise! He hath digged his own pit, and shall fall into it!"

O, deliver my soul from the glinting sword of the professional diplomat, who drippeth honey from his mouth and offereth up the fruits of my labor, though he laboreth not, **neither does he work.**

O, I am weary! My strength is dried up and thou art glad. For thou well-knowest that to make me weary, is to make me sleep. Yet thou knowest not that in my dreams I am as the hungry man who eateth...but when I waketh both my soul and belly art empty, and I have wolves' eyes.

Lo! Art thou surprised that the lamb who goeth to slaughter becometh a wolf in sheep's clothing?

For behold, the nations of the earth shall witness a great commotion, and thou shalt behold a fierce People; for the eyes of the sleeping shall snap open wide, and the feet of the oppressed shall march to their voting places. Yea, they shall come, and declare that unrighteous rulers art brought down and fallen, but the People are risen and once again shall stand upright among nations.

"Experience hath shewn, that even under the best forms of government those entrusted with power have, in time, and by slow operations, perverted it into tyranny."

—Thomas Jefferson

THE
BOOK OF KINGS

These two things causeth the pangs of
  indigestion; lo, one is cold chicken soup and
  the other is a ruler that hath two mouths; yea,
  one for this and the other for that. He is like
  unto the weather vane that waits to see which
  way the political winds bloweth; yea, he is a
  map that stringeth thee along in the circular
  route.

And it shall come to pass that thou shalt say to
  thyself, "Lo, I am walking in a rut, surely I
  have walked this way many times before; yea,
  this path feeleth more familiar than a past-due
  notice; yea, it remindeth me of my daily bills."

Then shalt thou grumble and fall out of line; and
  the king, who is far ahead of thee and beyond
  hearing, shall see the great dispersion among
  the People and grow fearful about his
  reelection.

Therefore he runneth scared and maketh friends
  with the rocks; sometimes he hideth inside

and sometimes he standeth upon them. Yea, from high up he calleth to thee, saying **whatsoever thing** that causeth thee to fall back into line.

Behold, he wanteth thy vote!

In all things, the king mocketh thee, saying: "There is no relationship." Then he thinketh better of it and so he admitteth, "Yea, there was one." Yea, kings art all the same, as one king sayeth, "Read my lips. No new taxes," another sayeth, "They hath weapons of mass destruction!" Yea, thou art made dumb by the contradictions that cometh after election and after the facts are known; yea, it is a dynasty of shock and woe.

Lo, it is good to be king, for no king will stand accountable for his double-talk; yea, he flattereth himself out of trouble. He promiseth more.

A King knoweth that honeycomb catcheth more flies than a vinegar sop, so he wooeth thee, saying: "If ye will yet follow me, I will make you a great nation once again!"

He blameth his condition on enemies and he
blameth thy condition on Congress; yea, and
they war without ceasing.

Yea, they squabble and tattle, they whine and
defame, they nurse their own interests and
have forgotten all else. The power of sensible
decision is not with any of them; not one will
stand accountable. The king hath no ability to
lead them, and they hath no ability to lead
themselves.

Lo, it is dangerous to their democratic future that
some of the people believeth, "We hath
followed this long, is it not better to trust in a
king that we know, rather than one we know
not?" How traveling in circles hath confused
them! Yea, they find the contradictions of
their loquacious king to be a fascinating thing.

Lo, the king sayeth whatsoever thing to sound
sure of himself, yet those who are wise will
hear between his lines and be not forgetful of
his few comings and many goings. His gilded
words which are void of substance are like
unto sour notes in a symphony: they ring not
true. Yea, he demandeth admiration from his

subjects for his lofty works abroad, but lo, he
is unto the nation as a potted plant is unto the
porch of a house: he *adorneth*.

The king is both a tail-wagging poodle and a
territorial pit bull: he ruleth like the first and
campaigneth like the second. Lo and behold!
these are in noways the same thing. The king
hath great cunning. He knoweth the power of
political slogans and he useth them without
ceasing. He sayeth, "protect our freedom,"
"protect our future," and "protect our
children" but know thou that slogans
serenade thine emotions. They meaneth
utterly nothing.

He leadeth the fat life and he protecteth his
moneyed bedfellows; yea, the king giveth
away perks to the richest among people.
When he is called into account for his actions
he waxeth indignant; yea, with strings of
words and non-answers he defendeth himself.

O, beware the king that whineth when the People
groaneth! For he is like unto a babe that
needeth much comfort when he wobbleth,
and many nannies to shore him up. Yea, he
weaveth proudly with a smile that runneth

over and will not scrub off. Yea, it is like unto the cheese on a dried dinner plate.

He is like unto the many rulers from ages past. He thinketh the intellect of the masses is a microscopic thing, but that their ability to forget is enormous. Yea, he swatteth idly at flies while he thinketh of his glory. In him, the People behold a Living Fairy Tale; for the Naked Emperor doth parade proudly, shewing off what does not exist, yea, he thinketh that because he sayeth something it is so; yea, many there are who doubt their own eyes and agree lamely with broadcast opinion.

Behold! The king breaketh oaths that he maketh, then he repenteth before the hour glass runneth out, and he commandeth the People to forgive him. Yea, the king is like unto the man who courteth a comely woman and voweth his allegiance, but when he hath wed her, he cavorteth with concubines and cometh not home.

Yea, he waiteth until the day of trouble to respond to the condition of the people; yea, in desperation he doth dangle a carrot; but like unto a perpetual procrastinator, he delivereth not the goods.

The king jetteth around on Air Force One to promote party interests and it costeth taxpayers fifty-six thousand shekels an hour. The king talketh much about what he hath done for his nation, but he hath taken the nation unto himself.

Behold, there are more sorrows than can be written; for this is an age in which Folly is drawn with cords of Vanity and economic disaster with a tight rope. Nevertheless, be not downcast, for though thy body worketh two jobs or worketh not at all, thy mind and soul cannot be owned. In this, there is hope of deliverance.

"If the freedom of speech is taken away then dumb and silent we may be led, like sheep to the slaughter."

—George Washington

THE
BOOK OF
PATRIARCHS

**The Fathers of Freedom Rage; hear them
thunder!** Their alarm echoes from shining sea
to polluted shore; from crime-infested streets
to ramshackle farms; from silent factories to
the racket of political double-talk; from the
White House to Capitol Hill; from the gaunt
faces of America's outcast to the smug faces of
America's aristocracy.

Yea, they pronounce sentence upon the heretics
who have corrupted the People's government
and the treasonous "leadership" that gives
patriotism lip service while America is given
away and collapses from within. They are
ashamed of the power mongers. They are
ashamed of the check–bouncing money-
rubbers who profess to be leaders. They are
ashamed of all the scandal which is yet to be
revealed—for under the tip of the iceberg,
there is a dark and secret continent.

And they appeal to every one of the People,
saying: Children of the Republic! Our beloved
America, land of the indebted and home of
the homeless! Think not thyself to be trapped
by the rulers that confound thee on all sides,
for in this illusion thou art like unto the
trained oxen enclosed by a circle of string.
They behold it, and believe they cannot
escape; yea, they remain huddled and
motionless while their masters mortar the
bricks that will lock them up tight.

Behold, a herd of oxen is a powerful
congregation to break down a string, but lo,
they hath been conditioned to forget their
native freedom and to respond to suggestion.
Yea, they are tame; they are considered by
their rulers as profit-making inventory.

Awaken, all ye People! Freedom is thine heritage
and was won by courage, dreams, hopes,
hardship, and blood. Thou art a powerful and
mighty congregation; therefore trample down
the string that falsely imprisons thee, lest one
day thou shalt be contained in a pit with high
walls.

54

Choose ye this day to govern yourselves; for
freedom won by sacrifice of life, is lost by
sacrifice of will. Therefore seek the leader!
Flee the ruler! The first one crieth to thee in
the wilderness, and the second one standeth
at democracy's door.

Behold, America . . .*his darkened shadow upon
thy floor.*

"Over grown military establishments under any form of government are inauspicious to liberty, and are to be regarded as particularly hostile to republican liberty."

—George Washington

THE
REVELATION
OF TRUTHS

Now in the fourth year of the reign of kings, there comes to pass the usual election upon the land; and while the stumping politicians grope for followers among the People, the People grope for a leader among the stumped politicians.

For behold, a leader is much needed; yea, even a good shepherd, for the People are likened to an unprotected flock of sheep whose weakened fringes are being hewn down by poachers. Yea, they perish from hunger and cold; they shed blood amongst themselves; many are ravaged by poverty, depression, drugs and despair.

From a distance, the world watcheth as even the strong are laid waste. Yea, even the huddled core is endangered; lo, the middle-class taxpayer is threatened with extinction.

From a distance, a New World Order looketh upon the internal unraveling of a fleeced flock that once roamed the earth as mighty and fat, but now groweth weak and lean. Yea, they are cannibalized by their own kind; they hath afflictions that threaten to vanquish them slowly—or to wipe them out quickly as by a deadly summer freeze.

From a distance, the same old politicians watcheth the carnage with a wary eye and a partisan heart. Lo, and behold! They agonize about reelection to their protected fortress of power while they intellectualize about the suffering they have created.

Yea, this is a time of decision. The People stand before a fork in the road of their destiny, and it shall not be the Right nor the Left that shall lead them into safety, for these have been marked by the highwaymen and robbers who beckon them into ambush. Awaken! for both the Right and the Left turn back into a circular path just beyond the People's view; yea, their oppressors hath planted new scenery to entice an exhausted flock into the same old rut.

Yea, the reigning powers hath dragged a famished People through potholes and ditches; yea, the status quo hath drawn a map of their conquest. Lo! The kind–and–gentle

People must learn to defend themselves; they must sacrifice the status quo before the status quo sacrifices the People upon an altar of arrogance, folly and greed.

Behold, an altogether new road must be forged, but the People are confused and without leadership. They speak among themselves, saying, "What choices are these? Yea, it is ever between two evils that we choose, for the bureaucrats hath us in a bind; yea, they are all alike and we are weary of it all." Behold, their fatigue hath made them sleepy. Many are not alert; yea, they are easy to trip.

And so it is, that the events which hath gathered them into servitude shall keep them there, unless they snap awake! Yea, they must exchange apathy for passion; they must reason for themselves; they must begin to divide truth from illusion. For only with quickened minds can the People separate the shepherd leader from the shepherd ruler.

Behold, the markings of each one are different. The leader is obscure and little-known, but the ruler is like unto a flashy lizard that attracteth its mate — and the land is plagued with countless of his kind. The ruler hath the character of a chameleon. He is a politician of changing shades who disguiseth himself as a leader because he lusteth to be king. Yea, to see the ruler for what he is, is to see him for what he is not.

The ruler lureth a certain kind of following. Yea, he needeth the perfect constituent. Followers who offereth up the scepter and throne to him are uncomplaining, like unto a trodden door mat; involved, like unto a hermit crab; inflammatory, like unto a wet match; enlightened, like unto a gopher hole; worshipful, like unto a praying pilgrim; agreeable, like unto a whipped hostage; yea, and above all, they are more generous than an evergreen money tree.

Yea, the ruler expects the People to love him for vices, to serve his interests, and to reelect him into the Great Beyond. In his puffed-up arrogance, he thinketh not himself to be accountable to those that have entrusted him — and he feeleth altogether justified in his lies. Yea, he hath the forked tongue of his species; his communication is clever and expert. Behold the great twist! When he speaketh, his twining words attempt to conceal and misinform, therefore he communicateth not at all.

Yea, the ruler is an expert at rhetoric, even though he condemneth it to make himself appear honest. He knoweth the impact of the emotional word and he useth it repeatedly. Yea, he useth "women", "rights", "freedom", "jobs", "children" and "economy" like a composer useth "forte", "andante" and "sustain" to create beautiful music. Yea, the ruler's words strike chords of feeling, but his acts are evidence of an instrument sorely out of tune.

When it comes to pass that the People knoweth the facts behind his words, they hath dark doubts between the promise and the event; therefore he playeth the game of rhetorical evasion. Yea, he diverteth the People continually! He sidesteppeth 'round the issues, but he speaketh like unto the point of a needle when he jabbeth his opponent.

The ruler hath soothsaying pollsters that tell him what the People wanteth to hear; therefore, he plotteth his speech! Yea, he sayeth whatsoever thing that will electrify human emotion and win him the vote! He appeareth to be alone, yet he hath invisible armies enlisted with corporate interests and hidden alliances; lo, he calleth these his "advisors." Hearken, kind and trusting sheep: until the ruler is crowned king and can bury his entire body into the public purse, they are the moneybags who empower him; they are the brains behind his contrived expertise. Yea, he hath mortgaged himself for a **white house**, and the People will pay his debts from the bottom of their empty pockets for generations to come.

The ruler is both a novice and a savant. He is a novice regarding the day–to–day life of the common man and his dignity; but he is a savant in his understanding of the common man's desire to be unburdened with government. Yea, theirs is a marriage of both implication and convenience, for rulers think of themselves as superior beings who have a calling to rule because the common man is viewed as unable to govern himself.

The ruler is well–oiled; he grinneth much. His powerful wizards study videos of his public performances to plot a better battle strategy; lo, they tell him how to hold his head before the camera! Yea, he is groomed by his handlers to the last eyelash in the ways of "electability." Lo! In him, the People behold a manufactured image that reflects the manipulation of democracy; it is a negative whereon is etched the fading picture of a government by the People; yea, it is a panoramic view of what might perish from the earth.

It is a sorry fact that some of the People will choose any ruler who promises to relieve them of their afflictions! Woe, woe unto them! They are as trusting babes in a den of venomous asps. Yea, the asps are fascinating! Behold them sway, to and fro! They beguile the Republic into a pit. They devour her one soul at a time; one voter at a time, and all apathetic nonvoters in one great gulp.

Verily, there is no ruler that can be trusted! There is no ruler that can save them. Their only deliverance is a government by the People and shepherd leaders to point the way. But behold, this is a solution so obvious that many overlook it; yea, many mistakenly believe that this is their system of government, when the truth, half-truths, and lies camped all around them is evidence of a former fact turned fiction. Yea, the crimes of their rulers are a slow poison—but the People's spell of illusion is concealed danger with a timing device.

For behold, many of the People have forgotten how to think; yea, they speak as if to figure solutions to their problems but their mouths are full of programmed slogans and popular reasoning; yea, even broadcast opinion.

And so it is possible that the People can be presented with a shepherd leader and reject him altogether; yea, the spell of illusion hath a strong grip. The People must snap awake! They must begin to howl, individually and with a unified voice. Yea, they must resist their fatigue and gather the strength to act.

For behold, the People have been run down by a system run astray, and it is a system that is locked up tight. Yea, they mourn because those who would be good leaders cannot get elected; yea, one worthy to lead them hath not four hundred million shekels to buy a job that pays two hundred thousand shekels a year. Yea, the People are walled-off from their government because it is dominated by the elite and powerful, by a befouled system of campaign funding and moneyed interests.

Yea, theirs is a system of government that was founded to serve the welfare of the many, but hath become instead a system of welfare for the rich. Yea, the good of the few — or of the one — has become the meat of legislation, the honey of territorial hornets and the milk of babes born to the rich and powerful. Yea, it is a system likened unto a sweet and juicy pomegranate which is rotten at its core.

Yea, and the People eat into the rot without flinching; yea, they eat as if they are drugged. The foul decay does not shock them, for they have been conditioned to tolerate bigger and bigger mouthfuls until their bellies are full of rot and utterly empty of sustenance.

Behold the hypocrisy of this elitist system in which the rulers make laws to prosecute criminals, but which allows these same lawmakers to commit criminal acts without reprisal!

Yea, with hypnotic rhetoric they bamboozle the public; they season their words to taste, they sugar the rot. Behold the ruse! Yea, the common citizen who commits illegal acts is hunted down and jailed; he is charged and sentenced but lo, the rulers debate about whether the powerful shall be charged. From the hill of lofty arrogance, they debate about whether to "trust the public" with a disclosure of truth. Yea, they vote whether or not to be prosecuted and in the end, they conspire to withhold incriminating evidence in the name of "public business," "national security," and the "public's right to a quick solution."

Yea, their consciences are seared as with a hot iron: they altogether stinketh with rot. Yea, they stand before the public as the scribes and Pharisees of old. They profess uprightness always; but inwardly, they are as whitewashed mausoleums, full of gangrene and defilement.

Yea, and all of this hath come to pass because the people hath slept the sleep of democracy's death; they hath been pacified during years of prosperity; they hath looked askance at progressive government infractions; they hath voted passively through the polls; they hath become easy to figure. Yea, their limits and tolerance hath been probed; their secrets are known; their defenses hath been slowly peeled away and unless they wake up and take charge of their country, they will lose their freedoms without ever going to war. Yea, and their children shall suffer untold pangs; they will labor under oppressive burdens that will grind their living into dust.

Behold the supreme folly of blind and stumbling rulers who froth and rave and vow to "keep America strong" as she is laid waste without musket, cannon or ballistic attack. They are without wisdom and utterly without mind. Behold an age in which people shall cry out for their deliverance; an age in which extreme conditions are fueled by "moderate," conformed thinking! Behold a nation founded upon principles of freedom and citizens who embrace willful unconcern as a mark of stability and sophistication! Behold a nation that pursues goods of every kind with a consuming frenzy, yet remains unmoved while it is utterly stripped of good government!

O, if the People could see through the intricate snare of rulers and powers! They would understand that the truth is mocked because the People are feared, for the powers know they have been caught too often. Yea, the rulers know that the masses could erupt in rage and contempt; yea, they know that truth giveth freedom and lies stealeth it away.

Lo, this is an unprecedented time in the history of a mighty nation founded upon the principles of freedom, justice, and equality — a time in which its survival is in crisis and is gasping for breath. Yea, let the Sons and Daughters of the Republic gather themselves together; for behold, the Truth of all things shall not be overcome.

Yea, the People's defense of Life, Liberty, and the Pursuit of Happiness is the hope of their deliverance, forever and ever, without end.

These are the times that try men's souls: The summer soldier and the sunshine patriot will, in this crisis, shrink from the service of their country; but he that stands it now, deserves the love and thanks of man and woman. Tyranny, like hell, is not easily conquered; yet we have this consolation with us, that the harder the conflict, the more glorious the triumph. What we obtain too cheap, we esteem too lightly: it is dearness only that gives every thing its value.

Thomas Paine,
from *The American Crises*, 1774

THE
BOOK OF PATRIOTS

**In all the ages of earth there was raised up
among Men** a season and a generation most
strong and wise and true. Yea, in our forebears
was the divine breath of sovereignty and the
heart of life itself, unto the toppling of rulers
that conceived all manner of mischief, whose
blood was made haughty from before recorded
ages, whose self-appointed task was to oppress
the poor and grind the spirit, to bring forth
falsehood and tyranny, unto the confining of
freedom, to bind it under authority forged in
irons, to mock and scorn the right of self-rule,
granted by Divine Providence unto all of
humankind.

In the tenth generation of Patriots that loosed the
bonds of kings and overthrew the mighty,
there cometh a grievous cry all across the land;
yea, for that which has always been could
always be; yea, there may be no new thing
under the sun.

For as in times of old, the leaders hath become as
   rulers, they hath brought forth mischief, they
   hath conceived falsehoods; yea, the tabernacle
   of political thievery doth prosper and they
   that rob the People art secure.

Lo! For like unto the days of their fathers, the
   People hath petitioned them that rule, saying,
   Hear the words of our mouths, O President,
   O Congressmen, O Representatives, O
   Governors, O Judges, O Mayors, O
   Councilmen! We beseech thee by day and by
   night. Thy words unto us are as the butter of a
   goat, yet thine hearts are like unto weapons
   against us.

Yea, thy promises and polished words pour out
   like the oil of an almond upon the thigh of a
   centerfold maiden; yet thine humility is like
   unto the consuming serpent, and thy
   purposes are set as swords against us.

For out of the city that is desolate our
   consolations are naught and the People art
   weary of thee; yea, many there say, leave us
   alone for we are wasted by flattery. Yea, thy
   mouths do testify against thee; lo, ye hath no
   remorse and conscience is not with thee.

For up from the tabernacles of bribery thou hast given us wrinkles, yea, thou hast hijacked the years of our youth and shortened the days of old age. We breaketh with burden. We partaketh of pills to comfort our minds; yea, we are epidemically depressed.

With the rod of the law do ye smite us, with our silver ye forge us to debt, thou hast covered our backs and cursed our wombs and our hair is become baldness. Yea, thou hast given thorns without meat and hemlock, without wheat.

We art empty in pocket, broken in mind, and **servants to the kingdom of wealth**.

Thou turnest our glory to shame.

But lo! All these things are not the worst of it, for thou hast strayed from our Constitution, the holy writ from which our democratic freedoms arise. Yea, the Constitution is the Ark of our sacred contract, bequeathed unto us before thou wast formed in the flesh. Yea, thou hast defiled the sacrosanct and made unto it a sandbox, even a playground for **evil-doers**, irreverent **imbeciles**, and intellectual **fools**.

73

Yea, O politicians, with thy ceaseless army of
sycophants, thou hast broken our laws, taxed
us without our consent, constrained our
fellow citizens, failed to protect our borders,
financed a multitude of police powers to
enforce the countless, burdensome laws thou
hast made for sport; thou hast obstructed
justice, failed to address matters of urgent and
pressing importance and hast brought forth
tyrannical agencies to make us subject. Thou
hast fundamentally altered our government,
tortured detainees, detained persons without
evidence, engaged in excessive secrecy, spied
on American citizens, handed to political
appointees unconstitutional and excessive
powers, and hath made the meaning of a
patriot unto one who is a **consort** of thine
oppression.

Yea, thou hast committed more offenses against
this people and their democratic republic than
can be written in this age, but thine offenses
art known in the secret places of life and they
shall be revealed in an hour soon to come, as a
scourge upon the forces of deception and
upon all the kingdoms of darkness.

74

Behold, the patriots of this nation love their
country, their land of promise and their
inheritance of liberty. And many among them
knoweth that remedy is with the People, not
with the polluted ones who govern without
common sense, without conscience, who are
hapless wizards behind a curtain of glory that
hideth an ashen crypt of consciousness.

Lo, their politicians and appointees are likened
unto the nation's executioners, who taketh
away tomorrow as the clock ticketh.

Yea, the People know by the dread in their bones
that their time runneth out, and from the holy
chamber of their spirits ascends a Sacred Fire
most righteously indignant. Yea, these are
men and women of Might and they are many
in number. Yea, for it hath come to pass that
the Patriots awaken as the Trumpets of
Destiny art sounded.

And the Trumpets of Destiny art seven, and they
art grievous.

The First Trumpet is named "Free Trade,"
heralded by a Duplicitous Duo, called by
double "i's" and triple "l's" that dodge

discovery and chronically anguish the nation; yea, and many wail their pestilent dirge.

The Second Trumpet is named "Deterioration," heralded by one cannibal with twin heads, called Two Political Parties.

The Third Trumpet is named "Corruption," heralded by Egomaniacal Elite.

The Fourth Trumpet is coded "Nine Eleven," heralded by a hemlock bush set about with chains, and to this is given no name for it is blotted from the Book of Liberty.

And the Fifth Trumpet is named "Desert Death," heralded from the core of an unholy black hole, by red-eyed, Fundamentalist Greed.

The Sixth Trumpet is named "Patriot Act," trumpeted by Treasonous Deceit.

And the Seventh of these is called "Economic Collapse," trumpeted by Robbers &Thieves.

Yea, the People awaken to this generation of political hypocrites who hath jaws unto knives and teeth unto swords, that seek to

devour the poor from the earth and the needy
from among men, in countless numbers and
by countless complicities. Yea, and shattering
trauma hath knocked the People in their
heads; yea, their crusted sores hath fallen off;
yea, the scales art gone from their eyes. They
seeth; yea, they heareth; and lo, goodly reason
is with them. They thinketh once again. And
all these things are harbingers to a coming
Age of Decency, wherein Liberty is lifted from
her heap.

And the People declare unto their politicians,
    saying:

The time is upon thee that We, the People, do
    hiss corruption out of high places and secrets
    out of low swamps; yea, and thou shalt
    deliver unto us our nation, straightaway.

For lo, if ye hath no trust in thine ability to
    represent the People and to keep our
    commandments, that ye cower like canines
    'neath the table of a king, get thee away from
    us! Thou canst then go to work and earn thy
    meat as an indentured servant, *like unto
    ourselves.* Yea, it is better to be as one of us,
    than to suffer the pangs of a vast villainy and

to be judged and sentenced for the multitude
of crimes yet to be revealed.

Yea, there is a great evil under the sun, and this is
the indifference of the politician for his
people. And all of this hath we learned from
history, that when a man crieth, "I am free!" it
was far from him. And we knoweth that
corruption must needs be plucked up by the
roots, else it prevail within hidden places, to
rise once again and choke the garden of
Liberty from the face of the earth.

Henceforth why should we live, if our
Democratic Republic be gone? We are a
People of Inheritance, and our land a legend
of bounty, filled to overflowing with wheat
and barley, honey and figs, and the many
waters of life.

We tilled the land and pitched us houses and
bore fruits for the good of the earth. We died
to be free. Yet, we hath fallen asleep in our
fatness; yea, and in our dream we groweth
sick and lean; yea, we awaken to a nation
bedeviled with scorpions and drought.

Lo in the wink of an eye, we shall rise to our feet, to sweep the land clean and till us a representative government. Yea, and apathy shall be no more, neither political corruption, neither tyrannical consolidation of power, neither trite division nor manufactured thought, neither sickness for profit, nor shackles of debt, nor deception, nor secrecy, nor militarism, nor injustice, nor oppression, nor fear, nor subservience, nor blindness, nor deafness, nor laden hearts that do not sing, nor lust for consumption, for the People shall be healed of national disease.

We shall live free to govern ourselves once again. Yea, we will rebuild our garden of Liberty like unto the patriots before us that begot us, that bled for us and builded for us, long time passing.

And this is not all, for we shall preserve, protect, and defend **one another**, for brotherhood is the force of nature within us. For it shall come to pass that when politics and philosophies die to our worship, the evils that divide men and breed their destruction shall swallow themselves up and a nightmare shall pass from the earth.

Yea, as the sun maketh its light, man's quest to go free is like unto the expansion of heaven, where tyranny hath no dominion. Yea, the sons and daughters of Liberty must needs remain; yea, and they shall be the **last ones standing.**

"Information is the currency of democracy. Whenever the people are well-informed, they can be trusted with their own government."
—**Thomas Jefferson**

THE
SOOTHSAYER SCROLLS

In the infancy of the 21st Century, the
technologies of Man advanceth; yea, it is the
Reign of the Gods of Information, and they
are many, and they are false. These are the
Gods of silken robes and well oiled lips that
shine as the rising sun upon a pond of fat
catfish in the **mourning,** seven days of every
week. And many of them art carved as unto
graven images of hand-rubbed wax; yea, and
they talk fastly without ceasing. Yea, and
these Gods are vain above all idols known to
man.

And lo, many there be that honor these
soothsaying Gods and believeth their
seductions; yea, and their prattling words
raineth down in digits, from high in the sky
near the stars do they come. Yea, upon
shining scrolls set into boxes the words of the
Gods art written and their voices art heard;
yea, the people hath named the high mass of

the Gods, and they calleth their ceremony, "The News. "

And lo, those among the people who worship these false gods are them that sleepeth while they walketh; yea, they are fashioned dumb to the light of day by the condescending ones they adoreth. Yea, and them that venerate before the scrolls hath minds that are scorched, like unto a burned harvest of wheat. Yea, the minds of those who bow down before the Gods are seared by foolishness, by frivolities and sophistries, by clever deceptions that the Gods weaveth, as a magician's spell is woven beneath a darkened moon.

But lo, not all the people worship blindly, for many among them art sorely vexed and they grieve. Yea, for it hath come to pass that the Gods hath gone drunk with giddy in so great a measure that only minds carved in marble cannot question the Gods lunatic ravings; yea their talk is certifiable; yea, it is clinically insane.

Yea, the sensible and wise among the people sayeth, "What is this meaningless talk?! Our journalists hath become models and movie stars and there is no information with any of them, let alone any truth. Yea, their heads are vacant and their words, gobbledygook. They hath elevated senseless speech to a most ridiculous glory. We are dumbfounded; yea, our tongues are tied with astonishment. Woe! What hath become of the news?"

Yea, the wise among the people art provoked to anger by vain and prattling faces with well set hair and mouths of polished pearls, children void of wisdom, not unto the coming of age. Yea, the people weary of the God's parroted talk, their insincere protests while injustice multiplies throughout the land, their pretended love of the people when they giveth no warning to save them, but performeth, instead. Yea, the people art revolted by their bubbly playacts upon a whitewashed stage; yea, the people utterly hateth their propaganda performance. And the wailings of the people do ascend like waves over the wounded body of Liberty, high unto the Creator of Life itself.

For while the vain Gods of Information stand high and aloft above the masses, the life of the nation and its Free Press hath become desolate; yea, from under the glittering pillars of pretense fainteth a nation, parched for Liberty's water of truth.

Yea, the People wander confused, for the journalistic wells hath gone dusty and dried, long time passing.

Yea, many among people knoweth not that in their Age of Information they hath been disinformed for ages. Yea, and while the mouths of the Gods art moistened by fine wine, the people hath tongues sorely cracked; yea, they perish of thirst for the justice that will save them.

Yea, while the people are wont for the democratic facts, they are indoctrinated instead; yea, they art coddled and coaxed, instructed and opined upon, told of celebrities and shown the First Lady's robes.

Lo and behold, when the big booms called headlines at last make a sound, they cometh in seconds and sound bites. Lo, the words that are spoken deflect or dispel; yea, the who, what, when, where, why, or how's art

covered up. Yea, the Information Gods
provideth a Spectacle of Witlessness, **laid
bare**.

Yea, the People behold the irony of an age when
words mean not what they mean, when
unrestrained speech is a crime, when it is
worse to offend than to suffer offenses, when
beauty is called ugly and that which is
hideous is held up for praise! When greed is
called good, and good is condemned, when
the lie is revered to be true.

Yea, before their eyes, the People behold a
shining, broadcast reality that holdeth them in
darkness while their democratic safeguards
hath been stolen away from before their
pried-open eyes. Yea, they behold a popular
press that is not a watchdog for the free, but
an outright mockery of American democracy;
yea, and it is utterly profane.

Yea, and their time to redeem themselves from
darkness is a mere grain of sand left into the
glass, for the moment of decision is upon
them now. Yea, and the only hope that
remaineth is for those among the people who
hath the gift of word and quill, to establish a

free and independent press in every city across the land.

For behold, Liberty sayeth to her nation, "Ye, the People must be wedded to the Truth in sickness and in health, 'till death do ye part. Let those of means and talent write new scrolls to inform the People, to save the nation, yea, to protect the life of democracy, to fearlessly inform."

Yea, true journalism is Liberty's army and those who deliver it are Patriots worthy of honor. Yea, they are enlisted by the Fathers of Freedom to the Worldwide Battle of Truth, to serve the People and deliver their Nation from a certain destruction, wrought by iniquitous secrets.

Yea, Freedom's Ring is the thunder of Truth, a mighty outcry for justice, a free Voice that feareth nothing and treadeth hard upon corruptors of a sacred Democratic Republic. Therefore, be not deceived and let freedom ring, for only the truth grindeth despotism to dust.

"Guard against the impostures of pretended patriotism."

—George Washington

THE
SONG OF DEMOCRACY

The Song of Songs, writ in the heart of the
People, at the beginning Portals of Time. Yea,
the sages of knowing hath kept secrets hid;
yea, to surprise the masters of slaves. Yea,
humankind shall be wrested from Powers and
rescued from Principalities, even redeemed
from Dominions and Thrones.

Yea, when hope fleeth away and the day become
dark, the People shall perish to falsehoods.
Time hath determined deception be known;
yea, and their sorrows shall topple to ruin.

And lo, an Epic of Joy shall follow the night of
the soul; yea, and a New Day cometh upon
them. Yea, instead of deception, there shall
come Truth. Instead of delusion, there shall
come Reason. Instead of a bloody divide,
there shall come a joyful Reunion.

For pollution shall be changed to purity, elitism
to equality, poverty to abundance, prattle to

reason, injustice to justice, law to conscience, sickness to health, arrogance to humility, greed to generosity, ignorance to knowledge, hatred to forgiveness, and all their fears shall be traded for love.

Yea, the People will choose goodness over goods, accountability over avoidance, nature over domination, self-expression over conformity, community over alienation, brotherhood over division, truth over belief, and conscientious action over apathetic lethargy.

Yea, the foundations of pure principle shall be their code of conduct and brotherly compassion their creed. Yea, change shall overtake the People and it shall be **their** change, by **their** design, by the power they hath within them.

For it shall come to pass that the common people shall govern themselves. Yea, and the farmer shall let fall his rake, the mechanic shall leave his garage, the geologist shall lay down his rocks, the physician shall shutter his practice; yea, and one, by one, by one, the People shall labor together to restore their Nation to Life.

And this is Democracy's Song:

Live free among the hills, rejoice within the
valleys, thou art blessed to roam the land, and
be made wholesome in the company of
strangers.

Fear not, for there is naught to fear. To every man
is given an equal measure, and to every
woman equal blessings and to every babe an
equal portion of his future, no prince and
paupers, here.

Prosper in joy and be generous for as ye give
unto others, it shall be returned unto thee.
Therefore be exceedingly glad, for there is
naught to bind thy progress.

Enlarge the dreams that hath woven thee, for thy
dreams art needful here. Therefore magnify
thy soul, for there is naught to bind thy
progress.

Share wisdom, speak truth, and lend thy life to
Liberty for thou art prized, O person, O pearl
of great price! Thereby make greater the
whole, for there is naught to bind thy
progress.

I am Democracy, the holy temple of human potential and destiny Divine! Protect me as I protect thee; as I enlarge thy life and bless thee indeed, to keep thee from kingdoms of darkness that you may not grieve. For man was made to know joy, and man was made to live free.

THE OATH OF
DEMOCRATIC
CITIZENSHIP

I.

I will preserve, protect, and defend the Constitution of the United States of America.

II.

I will be an empowered, self-determinant human being. I will accept personal responsibility and demand responsibility and accountability of leadership. I will work to empower a representative government.

III.

I will ask questions and demand truthful, direct and appropriate answers. I will discover the substance of issues. I will not look to any others, in any capacity, to shape my opinions. I will not mistake opinions for facts.

IV.

I will think. I will read. I will be informed.

V.

I will exercise my freedom of speech. I will speak out. I will participate. I will take action as appropriate. I will be unafraid of ridicule or intimidation. I will not go quietly into the night.

VI.

I will not vote the party line. I will not accept the inbreeding of power that is party politics. I will influence public and party policy with common sense, greater knowledge, my best intelligence and according to Constitutional principles.

VII.

I will not live in fear nor be tyrannized by fear. I will demonstrate courage to whatever extent it is called for, to protect this democratic republic, personal liberties, and to assure a just government.

VIII.

I will petition the government to uphold
Constitutional law. I will be alert to
infringements. I will demand that all
branches of government adhere to
Constitutional principles. I will protect
freedom and justice at all times.

IX.

I will not assume those in office will take
care of things. I will monitor government
and watch my representatives and officials
closely. I will not become apathetic or
ignore my responsibility for good
government at any time, even when the
economy is good.

X.

I will protect the rights of my neighbors.
Their rights are my rights, their welfare is
my welfare. I will support good citizens
who aspire to positions of public office in
order to be of service to all of us.

"Our country is now taking so steady a course as to show by what road it will pass to destruction, to wit: by consolidation of power first, and then corruption, its necessary consequence."

— **Thomas Jefferson**

EPILOGUE

"No problem can be solved from the same level of consciousness that created it."

— *Albert Einstein*

The underlying message in *The Ten Commandments of Political Office* is our democratic imperative to correct the balance of power in this nation. To preserve and heal our country — the social ground upon which our lives are built — we must come to understand the workings of power, what it is, where it resides, for what purposes it is used, and how it should be exercised.

While we think that most corruption in politics is about money, we fail to realize it's really about those in power, getting more. When those in positions of power get more, we get less.

What does power mean to you?

As a principle, power is not limited to worldly considerations: it is a spiritual essence.

Americans are generally not focused on the spiritual forces that sustain their lives behind the scenes of a brick-and-mortar reality. We prefer to take things at face value even when our material philosophies repeatedly injure us and so, most of us fail to realize that our declining national condition has occurred through the personal and collective power loss of common citizens.

On a psycho-spiritual level, protracted power loss manifests as illness. Are you, or is someone near to you, experiencing:

- Increased stress, anger, or fatigue?

- A need for psychotropic medications?

- Frequent physical problems?

- Loss of sleep? Anxiety or panic attacks?

- Depression?

- Addiction?

- Disintegration of personal relationships?

If so, you may wish to consider that power loss is a primary factor of this suffering. Socially oppressive conditions and the mind-set that permits this will manifest as ramshackle systems that weigh heavily upon those very people who look for external solutions to aid them, expanding personal and social dysfunction to epidemic proportions. While Americans have tended to move around obstacles created by the deteriorating social structures that we've

100

employed our government to manage for us, the system is so fouled now it is impossible to hide the condition of this country from the public... and for the public to run from the emerging facts.

Let's take a *very* brief look at what the government, its appointees and the officials employed with your tax dollars do to support your **Life**:

- Does the government wisely and rigorously regulate agencies that we pay to oversee public health and safety? Has the FDA protected your food and water? Your prescription medicines? What about other government programs and agencies, can you name their efficiencies and how you trust their oversight?

- Does the government oversee or regulate the economy in such a way that your finances are secure and is the dollar strong? Does it demonstrate good management of taxpayer monies? Does it assure that the SEC oversees and protects the public from corruption? That financial institutions and markets engage in fair business practices, without profit by usury and greed? That the American people are enabled to freely conduct commerce, have employment with acceptable wages so that they may acquire shelter, food, and the necessities of life?

- Does your government promote peace to assure American lives are not unnecessarily lost in war?

- Does your government answer demands for the health care needs of its citizens, a quality of care for the physical body? Are health care profits regulated so that health care is affordable for people?

Let's look at how government protects your **Liberty:**

- Do you remain current about legal developments that could impose limitations to your free speech, including Internet regulations proposed, or in the works?

- Are you subject to search without a warrant?

- Are you potentially spied upon by your government?

- Have you read The Patriot Act of 2001?

- If you have it, can you take a large sum of money out of the bank *this very day*? Tomorrow? When can you finally get your cash and what government agency is now the overseer of you possessing your money?

Let's take a glance at how the government stacks up in your **Pursuit of Happiness**:

- Can you be happy when you or someone you love is ill and you cannot get help?

- Can you be happy when there is a want of justice in the land? When powerful people can slide by the law, while average Americans cannot?

- Can you be happy with the burden of enormous public debt and unfathomable bailouts?

- Can you be happy when a loved one has died in a war...*begun as a lie*?

- Can you be happy when you lose your job and have no prospect for an acceptable one?

- Can you be happy when your hard-earned dollar is subject to evaporation any moment?

- Are you happy to pay exorbitant prices for necessities when corporations and executives gain record profits, *every quarter*? When they receive government funds, arrogantly claiming they are too big to fail, and then proceed to gain even *more* profit and *squander more cash* after picking taxpayer pockets?

- Are you unable to pursue happiness because there is no time in your life, due to work, excessive and unwarranted taxes, and a cost of living that keeps you on an unending economic treadmill?

Do you find that the actions (or inactions) of our government give you *more power* over your life... *or less*? Does this government Of, By, and For the People support your life, liberty, and the pursuit of happiness? If it does not, then what is it really doing? Why do we pay taxes? Why do we vote? Why do we believe we live under a democratic republic?

Perhaps we can see, however brief the lists, that the condition of the United States government has everything to do with our daily lives. We are not separate from government and we cannot hide.

So what is to be done?

Many believe we are nearly past hope, and they despair that people won't take action until it is too late. Yet, we must not overlook a sacred, mighty spiritual component in human beings that can—and has and will again—rise above oppression and misery because the darkness of those things is an affront to the Divine stuff that we are made of. Resistance to tyranny is inevitable, it as natural as the rain that lends life to the earth. The imperative, however, is when and how to take action, so that goodness will prevail and the promise of our lives will be preserved.

Before we can garner the collective power needed to save this nation, we must personally connect to the inherent power within our spiritual interior. This power is spirit, the taproot of Divine Consciousness, that ineffable connection to "Divine Providence" that our Founders firmly relied on. It is each person's inherent ability of intellect, will, choice, action, and responsibility: the *freedom* to be self-determinant individuals, whatever we aspire to achieve.

To reestablish the balance of power in our nation, we need the motivation that arises from the depth of need, so I ask you,

Would you take action to remedy human suffering if you knew you could do something about it?

Would you take action to reclaim this nation if you could know that your personal goodness has the right to good government?

Would you like to make an extremely positive difference in this world? —Do you have the sense that you were born with a special purpose?

Would you be better enabled to give of your love, your talent and ingenuity if life under current conditions were not so burdensome, so restricted by an unyielding, uninspired, and punishing system?

The freedom to achieve one's expansive potential is the essence of the American Dream, not merely an opportunity for prosperity. Although in this nation there should be no such thing as the "working poor" and no one should ever be without equal opportunity and ample necessities, the American dream is to live under the protection of a democratic society, with all the potential it affords to our lives.

On a spiritual level, oppression is the shadow side of power. Its egotistic impulse is to restrict, control and dismiss a person's innate capacity to be self-governing and free. Oppression and its extreme, tyranny, is enabled when people have only a limited sense—or no sense— of the power and inherent worth inside of them.

Whenever we permit others to do our thinking for us, to define truth for us, to entirely choose for us without our assent, or to confine our natural rights and thereby reduce our potential, we are not using our personal power. We are not self-governing. In a very real sense, we are not living free.

Freedom is bound to the imperative of responsibility, and contrary to what most people have been indoctrinated to believe, human beings are inherently decent and will express cooperative and life-affirming behaviors when impelled by a just society and educated with truth and reason. No one should be in a position of leadership without this understanding, for the essence of leadership is to bring out the best in human nature and to empower that.

Our society has skewed those organizational properties which would best serve our interests by lending the task of inspiration to religious powers and giving ourselves over to government for protection from everything. In both cases, personal power is surrendered and in both cases, there is a large failure to inspire the highest potential of humans to co-exist in mutuality and harmony. The failure of leadership to look after the interests of the collective is attributable to the fact that those who lead us are not spiritually enlightened, either. As we look for someone better, stronger, wiser to lead us...we will continue to be bitterly disappointed.

The one great leader we have all been waiting for is inside of us. **We are the ones we've been waiting for.** When we wake up to that truth, the external world will support our realization and decent, wise, expansive, and honest visionaries will come forth to represent the People they are a reflection of.

An Emerging World Government?

Beyond being citizens of this nation, we must be able to understand the faceted and critical reasons why our democratic republic must remain intact. Have you ever stopped to wonder what the world would have been like had a democratic America never been born? What it will be like if America passes? We should ponder this now.

There appears to be a subterranean movement towards a globalization of power. It appears that beautifully diverse human societies stand to become homogenized, much like the economic homogenization created by corporations around the globe: everywhere, a McDonald's, everywhere, Nestle products or Nike shoes. Whatever we believe about the unity of the human family, a homogenized, corporate-molded population, managed by a global power structure is not the way to achieve that.

A just government is based on leadership that will guide, support, and administer the affairs of its highly unique collective, as directed by the folks that built it. Its nemesis is a pyramidal power structure, where a few rule from the top down. These forms of government profess leadership, but that does not make it so. These are social systems that manage and control. And the bigger a government gets, the less capable of leadership it becomes.

We need to be careful about the agendas we are being teased into and remember that all puppies are adorable—and we think we want one—but when it grows into a vicious feral dog no one wants it then. Let us examine the pedigrees of their proposals and trace this to their origins. We will find some unwanted genetics and not necessarily the purity as purported.

There are strong indicators that the dismantling of American prosperity, set into high gear with the Clinton NAFTA deal, has been part of a long-range plan by the think-tank elite to install a global governmental operative. As America has been economically undermined, gradually and most recently by shock wave, we have been hearing pundits tell us Americans consume too much, we pollute too much, we are a general bane on the back of the planet.

Now it's appropriate that Americans are beginning to be conscientious about the environment and certainly, materialism has gotten the better of us. — But here again is another irresistible puppy. The *fact* is, people have been mercilessly indoctrinated by the powers-that-be to consume wantonly and to become indebted. The very people who steered, cajoled and advertised America into a mountain of debt and a materialistic frenzy are still doing that — while they simultaneously condemn us for polluting the planet and mock us as "financially irresponsible."

Certainly, it is necessary for human beings to come together but in no way does this mean that the United States of America, a democratic guard that has kept world tyranny in check, has to be bled of its prosperity for the good of the planet to occur. Quite the contrary.

Orwellian-style hypocrisy among the nation's elite is very fashionable and they engage in this without remorse. While trend-shaping, politically-connected and wealthy people seem to enjoy themselves taking turns at molding a new public humility for our own good, they are living very well, indeed. If what they promote is truly about principle and not about prompting your cooperation to enable their "we-know-what's-best" agenda, every single pundit who spouts about public policy to Americans will practice what they preach.

Double-talk is as common as it is abusive. Recognize it, and resist being manipulated by its confounding effects.

The Stockholm Syndrome and The Silence of the Abused Child

No matter how bad the condition of our nation becomes, Americans are loathe to confront their abusers. Some may be familiar with what is coined "The Stockholm Syndrome." It is recognized that hostages, unable to captain their fate and despite being tortured or otherwise abused, will become solicitous and even fond of their captors as a mechanism of psychological and physical survival. Examined another way, it is the syndrome of the abused child.

Abused children are notoriously silent. They shield their abusers, they experience shame at speaking out, they surrender in the hope that the bad things will stop, that by being compliant, they will survive, *somehow*.

If one is cognizant of the repeated disregard and the abusive actions toward the people of this nation by their narcissistic leadership, it is entirely appropriate to make comparisons to both hostages and abused children.

As empowered People of Destiny, let's give up our immature desires to be taken care of and cease to be passive about our government, hoping for justice in the face of abusive and chronic failures. Let us stop the pretense of being good citizens who are mute, looking the other way because it is assumed that average people are not supposed to look power in the eyes.

As long as governments are necessary, they must be allowed to exist for the well-being of the populace and thus, they must be governed. Not only must we look power in the eyes: **we must dare to stare.**

The founding patriots wielded a heretic philosophy and a treasonous world view. Their gestational leadership was the beginning of a promise for humankind that is now at risk of fading. Their legendary epiphany occurred over two hundred years ago, a stunning break from a

112

miserable philosophical paradigm based upon the so-called Divine Right of Kings.

The Divine Right of Kings and the Source of Repressive Governments

Even though red-blooded Americans scorn the fanfare, our media provides glitzy coverage of the British monarchy from time to time. We get media coverage, as well, of certain families happily referred to as "the American aristocracy," — with a subsequent awe being expected of us and an absurd promotion that certain families have a right to be in government because they are "special"...no other qualification necessary. We are likewise witness to a trend of unraveling mystic history where many people are fascinated by pharaohs, and led to consider claims that life's greatest secrets were known only by the hierarchical *"chosen ones."*

While at first this subject may seem irrelevant in a book about American freedom, it is very necessary to reveal how the wheat of truth gets mixed with the chaff of delusion. *Every single American needs to understand this as well as our Patriot forebears knew it: all men are created equal.* Let the elitists of this world have their vain parade and eat their cake, but leave our governance alone!

Our forebears *surrendered their lives* to rip apart from a reigning world view in which masses of people experienced oppression at the hands of the few who claimed they were chosen by their God to govern the masses. These societies were taught to believe that by superior lineage or superior force, some people are worthier than others. Furthermore, these diverse gods had a commonality which dictated that those who assented to "divine" agendas were to be favored and judged superior, those who did not, were inferior and to be condemned.

History reveals that societies which ascribe to this paradigm will experience a split between the favored and the outcast, fanning divisions that will reduce the potential of a unified human species to shreds. As Americans look to shape the greatest potential of this nation and blaze a trail for discovering yet another New World, let us remain aware of those unconscious assumptions borne of ageless beliefs that yet remain to be overcome.

A World Renaissance & The Newborn World

According to William James, "There is but one cause of human failure. And that is man's lack of faith in his true Self." There is a true Self inside of each one of us, an undiscovered country, a new frontier that is human Consciousness, waiting to be employed to our greatest end. We have not yet pried the cover off the powerful abilities we hide, inside. The critical circumstances of our world serve as the ultimate imperative that will force us into the discovery of our divine essence...the greatest of all truths which by its obfuscation has kept the entire human race enslaved to unending cycles of oppression and suffering.

At first, you may resist that idea with your mind, yet your heart tells you that you are good and powerful and that you can make a difference. —That you *must* make a difference. Listen to your heart...it holds the brilliance of a scintillating star...it is where love resides, and beauty, and compassion for your fellows and the genius of your being.

This world has a promising destiny, to be made of awakened, empowered humans. We can experience a New Day, the beginning of a New World that begins inside of each one of us. The unity of humankind is a given—it merely remains for us to recognize that, and embrace one another as equals. This is where we must start. And make no mistake, while we attend to the purification of our government, we are cleaning up the world and protecting its future as well.

As Thomas Jefferson said in his first inaugural address, let us do all the good in our power, "...to be instrumental in the happiness and freedom of all." Let us "...Advance with obedience to the work...and may that Infinite Power, which rules the destinies of the Universe, lead our counsels to what is best and give them favorable issue" for peace, prosperity, and the survival of our democratic republic.

"Lethargy is the forerunner of death to public liberty. The price of freedom is eternal vigilance."

—Thomas Jefferson

Part Three

THE
FREEDOM DOCUMENTS

"**P**rudence, indeed, will dictate that governments long established, should not be changed
for light and transient causes; and, accordingly, all experience abolishing the forms to
which they are accustomed. But, when a long
train of abuses and usurpations, pursuing invariably the same object, evinces a design to
reduce the people under absolute despotism, it
is their right, it is their duty, to throw off such
government, and to provide new guards for
their future security."

—**Thomas Jefferson**

THE
DECLARATION
OF
INDEPENDENCE

THE
DECLARATION
OF
INDEPENDENCE

JULY 4, 1776

When in the course of human events, it becomes
necessary for one people to dissolve the
political bands which have connected them
with another, and to assume among the
powers of the earth, the separate and equal
station to which the laws of nature and of
nature's God entitle them, a decent respect to
the opinions of mankind requires that they
should declare the causes which impel them
to the separation.

We hold these truths to be self-evident:

That all men are created equal; that they are
endowed by their Creator with certain

unalienable rights; that among these are life, liberty, and the pursuit of happiness; that, to secure these rights, governments are instituted among men, deriving their just powers from the consent of the governed; that whenever any form of government becomes destructive of these ends, it is the right of the people to alter or to abolish it, and to institute new government, laying its foundation on such principles, and organizing its powers in such form, as to them shall seem most likely to effect their safety and happiness. Prudence, indeed, will dictate that governments long established should not be changed for light and transient causes; and accordingly all experience hath shown that mankind are more disposed to suffer, while evils are sufferable than to right themselves by abolishing the forms to which they are accustomed. But when a long train of abuses and usurpations, pursuing invariably the same object, evinces a design to reduce them under absolute despotism, it is their right, it is their duty, to throw off such government, and to provide new guards for their future security. Such has been the patient sufferance of these colonies; and such is now the necessity which constrains them to alter their former systems of government. The history of the present King of Great Britain is a history of repeated injuries and usurpations, all having in direct object the establishment of an absolute tyranny over these states. To prove this, let facts be submitted to a candid world.

He has refused his assent to laws, the most wholesome and necessary for the public good.

He has forbidden his governors to pass laws of immediate and pressing importance, unless suspended in their operation till his assent should be obtained; and, when so suspended, he has utterly neglected to attend to them.

He has refused to pass other laws for the accommodation of large districts of people, unless those people would relinquish the

125

right of representation in the legislature, a right inestimable to them, and formidable to tyrants only.

He has called together legislative bodies at places unusual uncomfortable, and distant from the depository of their public records, for the sole purpose of fatiguing them into compliance with his measures.

He has dissolved representative houses repeatedly, for opposing, with manly firmness, his invasions on the rights of the people.

He has refused for a long time, after such dissolutions, to cause others to be elected; whereby the legislative powers, incapable of annihilation, have returned to the people at large for their exercise; the state remaining, in the mean time, exposed to all the dangers of invasions from without and convulsions within.

126

He has endeavored to prevent the population of these states; for that purpose obstructing the laws for naturalization of foreigners; refusing to pass others to encourage their migration hither, and raising the conditions of new appropriations of lands.

He has obstructed the administration of justice, by refusing his assent to laws for establishing judiciary powers.

He has made judges dependent on his will alone, for the tenure of their offices, and the amount and payment of their salaries.

He has erected a multitude of new offices, and sent hither swarms of officers to harass our people and eat out their substance.

He has kept among us, in times of peace, standing armies, without the consent of our legislatures.

He has affected to render the military independent of, and superior to, the civil power.

He has combined with others to subject us to a jurisdiction foreign to our Constitution and unacknowledged by our laws, giving his assent to their acts of pretended legislation:

For quartering large bodies of armed troops among us;

For protecting them, by a mock trial, from punishment for any murders which they should commit on the inhabitants of these states;

For cutting off our trade with all parts of the world;

For imposing taxes on us without our consent;

For depriving us, in many cases, of the benefits of trial by jury;

For transporting us beyond seas, to be tried for pretended offenses;

For abolishing the free system of English laws in a neighboring province, establishing therein an arbitrary government, and enlarging its boundaries, so as to render it at once an example and fit instrument for introducing the same absolute rule into these colonies;

For taking away our charters, abolishing our most valuable laws, and altering fundamentally the forms of our governments;

For suspending our own legislatures, and declaring themselves invested with power to legislate for us in all cases whatsoever.

He has abdicated government here, by declaring us out of his protection and waging war against us.

He has plundered our seas, ravaged our coasts, burned our towns, and destroyed the lives of our people.

He is at this time transporting large armies of foreign mercenaries to complete the works of death, desolation, and tyranny already begun with circumstances of cruelty and perfidy scarcely paralleled in the most barbarous ages, and totally unworthy the head of a civilized nation.

He has constrained our fellow-citizens, taken captive on the high seas, to bear arms against their country, to become the executioners of their friends and brethren, or to fall themselves by their hands.

He has excited domestic insurrection among us, and has endeavored to bring on the inhabitants of our frontiers the merciless Indian savages, whose known rule of warfare is an undistinguished destruction of all ages, sexes, and conditions.

In every stage of these oppressions we have petitioned for redress in the most humble terms; our repeated petitions have been answered only by repeated injury. A prince, whose character is thus marked by every act which may define a tyrant, is unfit to be the ruler of a free people.

Nor have we been wanting in our attentions to our British brethren. We have warned them, from time to time, of attempts by their legislature to extend an unwarrantable jurisdiction over us. We have reminded them of the circumstances of our emigration and settlement here. We have appealed to their native justice and magnanimity; and we have conjured them, by the ties of our common kindred, to disavow these usurpations which would inevitably interrupt our connections and correspondence. They too, have been deaf to the voice of justice and of consanguinity. We must, therefore, acquiesce in the necessity which denounces our separation, and hold them as we hold the rest of mankind, enemies in war, in peace friends.

We, therefore, the representatives of the United States of America, in General Congress assembled, appealing to the Supreme Judge of the world for the rectitude of our intentions, do, in the name and by the authority of the good people of these colonies solemnly publish and declare, That these United Colonies are, and of right ought to be, FREE

AND INDEPENDENT STATES; that they are absolved from all allegiance to the British crown and that all political connection between them and the state of Great Britain is, and ought to be, totally dissolved; and that, as free and independent states, they have full power to levy war, conclude peace, contract alliances, establish commerce, and do all other acts and things which independent states may of right do. And for the support of this declaration, with a firm reliance on the protection of Divine Providence, we mutually pledge to each other our lives, our fortunes, and our sacred honor.

John Hancock

Josiah Bartlett, Wm. Whipple, Saml. Adams, John Adams, Robt. Treat Paine, Elbridge Gerry, Step. Hokins, William Ellery, Roger Sherman, Samuel Huntington, Wm. Williams, Oliver Wolcott, Matthew Thornton, Wm. Floyd, Phil. Livingston, Frans. Lewis, Lewis Morris, Richd. Stockton, Jno. Itherspoon, Fras. Hopkinson, John Hart, Abra. Clark, Robt. Morris, Benjamin Rush, Benja. Franklin, John Morton, Geo. Clymer, Jas. Smith, Geo. Taylor, James Wilson, Geo. Ross, Caesar Rodney, Geo. Read, Tho. M'Kean, Samuel Chase, Wm. Paca, Thos. Stone, Charles Carroll, George Wythe, Richard Henry Lee, Th. Jefferson, Benja. Harrison, Ths. Nelson, Jr., Francis Lightfoot Lee, Carter Braxton, Wm. Hooper, Joseph Hewes, John Penn, Edward Rutledge, Thos. Hayward, Junr., Thomas Lynch, Junr., Arthur Middleton, Button Gwinnett, Lyman Hall, Geo. Walton

IN CONGRESS. JULY 4, 1776.

The unanimous Declaration of the thirteen united States of America,

"Don't interfere with anything in the Constitution. That must be maintained, for it is the only safeguard of our liberties."

"We the people are the rightful masters of both Congress and the courts, not to overthrow the Constitution but to overthrow the men who pervert the Constitution.

—Abraham Lincoln

THE
CONSTITUTION
OF THE
UNITED STATES
OF AMERICA

THE
CONSTITUTION
OF THE
UNITED STATES
OF AMERICA

We the people of the United States, in order to
form a more perfect union, establish justice,
insure domestic tranquility, provide for the
common defense, promote the general
welfare, and secure the blessings of liberty
to ourselves and our posterity, do ordain and
establish this Constitution for the United
States of America.

Article I

Section 1. All legislative powers herein
granted shall be vested in a Congress of
the United States, which shall consist of a
Senate and House of Representatives.

Section 2. The House of Representatives shall be composed of members chosen every second year by the people of the several states, and the electors in each state shall have the qualifications requisite for electors of the most numerous branch of the state legislature.

No person shall be a Representative who shall not have attained to the age of twenty five years, and been seven years a citizen of the United States, and who shall not, when elected, be an inhabitant of that state in which he shall be chosen.

Representatives and direct taxes shall be apportioned among the several states which may be included within this union, according to their respective numbers, which shall be determined by adding to the whole number of free persons, including those bound to service for a term of years, and excluding Indians not taxed, three fifths of all other Persons. The actual Enumeration shall be made within three years after the first meeting of the Congress of the United States, and within every subsequent term of ten years, in such manner as they shall by law direct. The number of Representatives shall not exceed one for every thirty thousand, but each state shall have at least one Representative; and until such enumeration shall be made, the state of New Hampshire shall be entitled to chuse three, Massachusetts eight, Rhode Island and Providence Plantations one, Connecticut five, New York six, New Jersey four, Pennsylvania eight, Delaware one, Maryland six, Virginia ten, North Carolina five, South Carolina five, and Georgia three.

When vacancies happen in the Representation from any state, the executive authority thereof shall issue writs of election to fill such vacancies.

The House of Representatives shall choose their speaker and other officers; and shall have the sole power of impeachment.

Section 3. The Senate of the United States shall be composed of two Senators from each state, chosen by the legislature thereof, for six years; and each Senator shall have one vote.

Immediately after they shall be assembled in consequence of the first election, they shall be divided as equally as may be into three classes. The seats of the Senators of the first class shall be vacated at the expiration of the second year, of the second class at the expiration of the fourth year, and the third class at the expiration of the sixth year, so that one third may be chosen every second year; and if vacancies happen by resignation, or otherwise, during the recess of the legislature of any state, the executive thereof may make temporary appointments until the next meeting of the legislature, which shall then fill such vacancies.

No person shall be a Senator who shall not have attained to the age of thirty years, and been nine years a citizen of the United States and who shall not, when elected, be an inhabitant of that state for which he shall be chosen.

The Vice President of the United States shall be President of the Senate, but shall have no vote, unless they be equally divided.

The Senate shall choose their other officers, and also a President pro tempore, in the absence of the Vice President, or when he shall exercise the office of President of the United States.

The Senate shall have the sole power to try all impeachments. When sitting for that purpose, they shall be on oath or affirmation. When the President of the United States is tried, the

Chief Justice shall preside: And no person shall be convicted without the concurrence of two thirds of the members present.

Judgment in cases of impeachment shall not extend further than to removal from office, and disqualification to hold and enjoy any office of honor, trust or profit under the United States: but the party convicted shall nevertheless be liable and subject to indictment, trial, judgment and punishment, according to law.

Section 4. The times, places and manner of holding elections for Senators and Representatives, shall be prescribed in each state by the legislature thereof; but the Congress may at any time by law make or alter such regulations, except as to the places of choosing Senators.

The Congress shall assemble at least once in every year, and such meeting shall be on the first Monday in December, unless they shall by law appoint a different day.

Section 5. Each House shall be the judge of the elections, returns and qualifications of its own members, and a majority of each shall constitute a quorum to do business; but a smaller number may adjourn from day to day, and may be authorized to compel the attendance of absent members, in such manner, and under such penalties as each House may provide.

Each House may determine the rules of its proceedings, punish its members for disorderly behavior, and, with the concurrence of two thirds, expel a member.

Each House shall keep a journal of its proceedings, and from time to time publish the same, excepting such parts as may in their judgment require secrecy; and the yeas and nays of the members of either House on any question shall, at the desire of one fifth of those present, be entered on the journal.

Neither House, during the session of Congress, shall, without the consent of the other, adjourn for more than three days, nor to any other place than that in which the two Houses shall be sitting.

Section 6. The Senators and Representatives shall receive a compensation for their services, to be ascertained by law, and paid out of the treasury of the United States. They shall in all cases, except treason, felony and breach of the peace, be privileged from arrest during their attendance at the session of their respective Houses, and in going to and returning from the same; and for any speech or debate in either House, they shall not be questioned in any other place.

No Senator or Representative shall, during the time for which he was elected, be appointed to any civil office under the authority of the United States, which shall have been created, or the emoluments whereof shall have been increased during such time: and no person holding any office under the United States, shall be a member of either House during his continuance in office.

Section 7. All bills for raising revenue shall originate in the House of Representatives; but the Senate may propose or concur with amendments as on other Bills.

Every bill which shall have passed the House of Representatives and the Senate, shall, before it become a law, be presented to the President of the United States; if he approve he shall sign it, but if not he shall return it, with his objections to that House in which it shall have originated, who shall enter the objections at large on their journal, and proceed to reconsider it. If after such reconsideration two thirds of that House shall agree to pass the bill, it shall be sent, together with the objections, to the other House, by which it shall likewise be reconsidered, and if approved by two thirds of that House, it shall become a law. But in all such cases the votes of both Houses shall be determined by yeas and nays, and the names of the persons voting for and against the bill shall be entered on the journal of each House respectively. If any bill shall not be returned by the President within ten days (Sundays excepted) after it shall have been presented to him, the same shall be a law, in like manner as if he had signed it, unless the Congress by their adjournment prevent its return, in which case it shall not be a law.

Every order, resolution, or vote to which the concurrence of the Senate and House of Representatives may be necessary (except on a question of adjournment) shall be presented to the President of the United States; and before the same shall take effect, shall be approved by him, or being disapproved by him, shall be repassed by two thirds of the Senate and House of Representatives, according to the rules and limitations prescribed in the case of a bill.

Section 8. The Congress shall have power to lay and collect taxes, duties, imposts and excises, to pay the debts and provide for the common defense and general welfare of the United States; but all duties, imposts and excises shall be uniform throughout the United States;

To borrow money on the credit of the United States;

To regulate commerce with foreign nations, and among the several states, and with the Indian tribes;

To establish a uniform rule of naturalization, and uniform laws on the subject of bankruptcies throughout the United States;

To coin money, regulate the value thereof, and of foreign coin, and fix the standard of weights and measures;

To provide for the punishment of counterfeiting the securities and current coin of the United States;

To establish post offices and post roads;

To promote the progress of science and useful arts, by securing for limited times to authors and inventors the exclusive right to their respective writings and discoveries;

To constitute tribunals inferior to the Supreme Court;

To define and punish piracies and felonies committed on the high seas, and offenses against the law of nations;

To declare war, grant letters of marque and reprisal, and make rules concerning captures on land and water;

To raise and support armies, but no appropriation of money to that use shall be for a longer term than two years;

To provide and maintain a navy;

To make rules for the government and regulation of the land and naval forces;

To provide for calling forth the militia to execute the laws of the union, suppress insurrections and repel invasions;

To provide for organizing, arming, and disciplining, the militia, and for governing such part of them as may be employed in the service of the United States, reserving to the states respectively, the appointment of the officers, and the authority of training the militia according to the discipline prescribed by Congress;

To exercise exclusive legislation in all cases whatsoever, over such District (not exceeding ten miles square) as may, by cession of particular states, and the acceptance of Congress, become the seat of the government of the United States, and to exercise like authority over all places purchased by the consent of the legislature of the state in which the same shall be, for the erection of forts, magazines, arsenals, dockyards, and other needful buildings;--And

To make all laws which shall be necessary and proper for carrying into execution the foregoing powers, and all other powers vested by this Constitution in the government of the United States, or in any department or officer thereof.

Section 9. The migration or importation of such persons as any of the states now existing shall think proper to admit, shall not be prohibited by the Congress prior to the year one thousand eight hundred and eight, but a tax or duty may be imposed on such importation, not exceeding ten dollars for each person.

The privilege of the writ of habeas corpus shall not be suspended, unless when in cases of rebellion or invasion the public safety may require it.

No bill of attainder or ex post facto Law shall be passed.

No capitation, or other direct, tax shall be laid, unless in proportion to the census or enumeration herein before directed to be taken.

No tax or duty shall be laid on articles exported from any state.

No preference shall be given by any regulation of commerce or revenue to the ports of one state over those of another: nor shall vessels bound to, or from, one state, be obliged to enter, clear or pay duties in another.

No money shall be drawn from the treasury, but in consequence of appropriations made by law; and a regular statement and account of receipts and expenditures of all public money shall be published from time to time.

No title of nobility shall be granted by the United States: and no person holding any office of profit or trust under them, shall, without the consent of the Congress, accept of any present, emolument, office, or title, of any kind whatever, from any king, prince, or foreign state.

Section 10. No state shall enter into any treaty, alliance, or confederation; grant letters of marque and reprisal; coin money; emit bills of credit; make anything but gold and silver coin a tender in payment of debts; pass any bill of attainder, ex post facto law, or law impairing the obligation of contracts, or grant any title of nobility.

No state shall, without the consent of the Congress, lay any imposts or duties on imports or exports, except what may be absolutely necessary for executing it's inspection laws: and the net produce of all duties and imposts, laid by any state on imports or exports, shall be for the use of the treasury of the United States; and all such laws shall be subject to the revision and control of the Congress.

No state shall, without the consent of Congress, lay any duty of tonnage, keep troops, or ships of war in time of peace, enter into any agreement or compact with another state, or with a foreign power, or engage in war, unless actually invaded, or in such imminent danger as will not admit of delay.

Article II

Section 1. The executive power shall be vested in a President of the United States of America. He shall hold his office during the term of four years, and, together with the Vice President, chosen for the same term, be elected, as follows:

Each state shall appoint, in such manner as the Legislature thereof may direct, a number of electors, equal to the whole number of Senators and Representatives to which the State may be entitled in the Congress: but no Senator or Representative, or person holding an office of trust or profit under the United States, shall be appointed an elector.

The electors shall meet in their respective states, and vote by ballot for two persons, of whom one at least shall not be an inhabitant of the same state with themselves. And they shall make a list of all the persons voted for, and of the number of votes for each; which list they shall sign and certify, and transmit sealed to the seat of the government of the United

States, directed to the President of the Senate. The President of the Senate shall, in the presence of the Senate and House of Representatives, open all the certificates, and the votes shall then be counted. The person having the greatest number of votes shall be the President, if such number be a majority of the whole number of electors appointed; and if there be more than one who have such majority, and have an equal number of votes, then the House of Representatives shall immediately choose by ballot one of them for President; and if no person have a majority, then from the five highest on the list the said House shall in like manner choose the President. But in choosing the President, the votes shall be taken by States, the representation from each state having one vote; A quorum for this purpose shall consist of a member or members from two thirds of the states, and a majority of all the states shall be necessary to a choice. In every case, after the choice of the President, the person having the greatest number of votes of the electors shall be the Vice President. But if there should remain two or more who have equal votes, the Senate shall choose from them by ballot the Vice President.

151

The Congress may determine the time of choosing the electors, and the day on which they shall give their votes; which day shall be the same throughout the United States.

No person except a natural born citizen, or a citizen of the United States, at the time of the adoption of this Constitution, shall be eligible to the office of President; neither shall any person be eligible to that office who shall not have attained to the age of thirty five years, and been fourteen Years a resident within the United States.

In case of the removal of the President from office, or of his death, resignation, or inability to discharge the powers and duties of the said office, the same shall devolve on the Vice President, and the Congress may by law provide for the case of removal, death, resignation or inability, both of the President and Vice President, declaring what officer shall then act as President, and such officer shall act accordingly, until the disability be removed, or a President shall be elected.

The President shall, at stated times, receive for his services, a compensation, which shall neither be increased nor diminished during the period for which he shall have been elected, and he shall not receive within that period any other emolument from the United States, or any of them.

Before he enter on the execution of his office, he shall take the following oath or affirmation:-- "I do solemnly swear (or affirm) that I will faithfully execute the office of President of the United States, and will to the best of my ability, preserve, protect and defend the Constitution of the United States."

Section 2. The President shall be commander in chief of the Army and Navy of the United States, and of the militia of the several states, when called into the actual service of the United States; he may require the opinion, in writing, of the principal officer in each of the executive departments, upon any subject relating to the duties of their respective offices, and he shall have power to grant reprieves and pardons for offenses against the United States, except in cases of impeachment.

He shall have power, by and with the advice and consent of the Senate, to make treaties, provided two thirds of the Senators present concur; and he shall nominate, and by and with the advice and consent of the Senate, shall appoint ambassadors, other public ministers and consuls, judges of the Supreme Court, and all other officers of the United States, whose appointments are not herein otherwise provided for, and which shall be established by law: but the Congress may by law vest the appointment of such inferior officers, as they think proper, in the President alone, in the courts of law, or in the heads of departments.

The President shall have power to fill up all vacancies that may happen during the recess of the Senate, by granting commissions which shall expire at the end of their next session.

Section 3. He shall from time to time give to the Congress information of the state of the union, and recommend to their consideration such measures as he shall judge necessary and expedient; he may, on extraordinary occasions, convene both Houses, or either of them, and in case of disagreement between them, with respect to the time of adjournment, he may adjourn them to such time as he shall think proper; he shall receive ambassadors and other public ministers; he shall take care that the laws be faithfully executed, and shall commission all the officers of the United States.

Section 4. The President, Vice President and all civil officers of the United States, shall be removed from office on impeachment for, and conviction of, treason, bribery, or other high crimes and misdemeanors.

Article III

Section 1. The judicial power of the United States, shall be vested in one Supreme Court, and in such inferior courts as the Congress may from time to time ordain and establish. The judges, both of the supreme and inferior courts, shall hold their offices during good behaviour, and shall, at stated times, receive for their services, a compensation, which shall not be diminished during their continuance in office.

Section 2. The judicial power shall extend to all cases, in law and equity, arising under this Constitution, the laws of the United States, and treaties made, or which shall be made, under their authority;--to all cases affecting ambassadors, other public ministers and consuls;--to all cases of admiralty and maritime jurisdiction;--to controversies to which the United States shall be a party;--to controversies between two or more states;--between a state and citizens of another state;--between citizens of different states;--between citizens of the same state claiming lands under grants of different states, and between a state, or the citizens thereof, and foreign states, citizens or subjects.

In all cases affecting ambassadors, other public ministers and consuls, and those in which a state shall be party, the Supreme Court shall have original jurisdiction. In all the other cases before mentioned, the Supreme Court shall have appellate jurisdiction, both as to law and fact, with such exceptions, and under such regulations as the Congress shall make.

The trial of all crimes, except in cases of impeachment, shall be by jury; and such trial shall be held in the state where the said crimes shall have been committed; but when not committed within any state, the trial shall be at such place or places as the Congress may by law have directed.

Section 3. Treason against the United States, shall consist only in levying war against them, or in adhering to their enemies, giving them aid and comfort. No person shall be convicted of treason unless on the testimony of two witnesses to the same overt act, or on confession in open court.

The Congress shall have power to declare the punishment of treason, but no attainder of treason shall work corruption of blood, or forfeiture except during the life of the person attainted.

Article IV

Section 1. Full faith and credit shall be given in each state to the public acts, records, and judicial proceedings of every other state. And the Congress may by general laws prescribe the manner in which such acts, records, and proceedings shall be proved, and the effect thereof.

Section 2. The citizens of each state shall be entitled to all privileges and immunities of citizens in the several states.

A person charged in any state with treason, felony, or other crime, who shall flee from justice, and be found in another state, shall on demand of the executive authority of the state from which he fled, be delivered up, to be removed to the state having jurisdiction of the crime.

No person held to service or labor in one state, under the laws thereof, escaping into another, shall, in consequence of any law or regulation therein, be discharged from such service or labor, but shall be delivered up on claim of the party to whom such service or labor may be due.

Section 3. New states may be admitted by the Congress into this union; but no new states shall be formed or erected within the jurisdiction of any other state; nor any state be formed by the junction of two or more states, or parts of states, without the consent of the legislatures of the states concerned as well as of the Congress.

The Congress shall have power to dispose of and make all needful rules and regulations respecting the territory or other property belonging to the United States; and nothing in this Constitution shall be so construed as to prejudice any claims of the United States, or of any particular state.

Section 4. The United States shall guarantee to every state in this union a republican form of government, and shall protect each of them against invasion; and on application of the legislature, or of the executive (when the legislature cannot be convened) against domestic violence.

Article V

The Congress, whenever two thirds of both houses shall deem it necessary, shall propose amendments to this Constitution, or, on the application of the legislatures of two thirds of the several states, shall call a convention for proposing amendments, which, in either case, shall be valid to all intents and purposes, as part of this Constitution, when ratified by the legislatures of three fourths of the several states, or by conventions in three fourths thereof, as the one or the other mode of ratification may be proposed by the Congress; provided that no amendment which may be made prior to the year one thousand eight hundred and eight shall in any manner affect the first and fourth clauses in the ninth section of the first article; and that no state, without its consent, shall be deprived of its equal suffrage in the Senate.

Article VI

All debts contracted and engagements entered into, before the adoption of this Constitution, shall be as valid against the United States under this Constitution, as under the Confederation.

This Constitution, and the laws of the United States which shall be made in pursuance thereof; and all treaties made, or which shall be made, under the authority of the United States, shall be the supreme law of the land; and the judges in every state shall be bound thereby, anything in the Constitution or laws of any State to the contrary notwithstanding.

The Senators and Representatives before mentioned, and the members of the several state legislatures, and all executive and judicial officers, both of the United States and of the several states, shall be bound by oath or affirmation, to support this Constitution; but no religious test shall ever be required as a qualification to any office or public trust under the United States.

Article VII

The ratification of the conventions of nine states, shall be sufficient for the establishment of this

Constitution between the states so ratifying the same.

Done in convention by the unanimous consent of the states present the seventeenth day of September in the year of our Lord one thousand seven hundred and eighty seven and of the independence of the United States of America the twelfth. In witness whereof We have hereunto subscribed our Names,

G. Washington - Presidt. and deputy from Virginia
New Hampshire: John Langdon, Nicholas Gilman
Massachusetts: Nathaniel Gorham, Rufus King
Connecticut: Wm: Saml. Johnson, Roger Sherman
New York: Alexander Hamilton
New Jersey: Wil: Livingston, David Brearly, Wm. Paterson, Jona: Dayton
Pennsylvania: B. Franklin, Thomas Mifflin, Robt. Morris, Geo. Clymer, Thos. FitzSimons, Jared Ingersoll, James Wilson, Gouv Morris
Delaware: Geo: Read, Gunning Bedford jun, John Dickinson, Richard Bassett, Jaco: Broom
Maryland: James McHenry, Dan of St Thos. Jenifer, Danl Carroll
Virginia: John Blair--, James Madison Jr.
North Carolina: Wm. Blount, Richd. Dobbs Spaight, Hu Williamson
South Carolina: J. Rutledge, Charles Cotesworth Pinckney, Charles Pinckney, Pierce Butler
Georgia: William Few, Abr Baldwin

"Our defense is in the preservation of the spirit which prizes liberty as a heritage of all men, in all lands, everywhere. Destroy this spirit and you have planted the seeds of despotism around your own doors.."

— Abraham Lincoln

THE
BILL OF RIGHTS

THE
BILL OF RIGHTS

Amendment I

Congress shall make no law respecting an
establishment of religion, or prohibiting the free
exercise thereof; or abridging the freedom of
speech, or of the press; or the right of the people
peaceably to assemble, and to petition the
government for a redress of grievances.

Amendment II

A well regulated militia, being necessary to the security
of a free state, the right of the people to keep and
bear arms, shall not be infringed.

Amendment III

No soldier shall, in time of peace be quartered in any
house, without the consent of the owner, nor in
time of war, but in a manner to be prescribed by
law.

Amendment IV

The right of the people to be secure in their persons, houses, papers, and effects, against unreasonable searches and seizures, shall not be violated, and no warrants shall issue, but upon probable cause, supported by oath or affirmation, and particularly describing the place to be searched, and the persons or things to be seized.

Amendment V

No person shall be held to answer for a capital, or otherwise infamous crime, unless on a presentment or indictment of a grand jury, except in cases arising in the land or naval forces, or in the militia, when in actual service in time of war or public danger; nor shall any person be subject for the same offense to be twice put in jeopardy of life or limb; nor shall be compelled in any criminal case to be a witness against himself, nor be deprived of life, liberty, or property, without due process of law; nor shall private property be taken for public use, without just compensation.

Amendment VI

In all criminal prosecutions, the accused shall enjoy the right to a speedy and public trial, by an impartial jury of the state and district wherein the crime shall have been committed, which district shall have been previously ascertained by law, and to be informed of the nature and cause of the accusation; to be confronted with the witnesses against him; to have compulsory process for obtaining witnesses in his favor, and to have the assistance of counsel for his defense.

Amendment VII

In suits at common law, where the value in controversy shall exceed twenty dollars, the right of trial by jury shall be preserved, and no fact tried by a jury, shall be otherwise reexamined in any court of the United States, than according to the rules of the common law.

Amendment VIII

Excessive bail shall not be required, nor excessive fines imposed, nor cruel and unusual punishments inflicted.

Amendment IX

The enumeration in the Constitution, of certain rights, shall not be construed to deny or disparage others retained by the people.

Amendment X

The powers not delegated to the United States by the
Constitution, nor prohibited by it to the states, are
reserved to the states respectively, or to the people.

"America will never be destroyed from the outside. If we falter and lose our freedoms, it will be because we destroyed ourselves."

— Abraham Lincoln

Part Four

PARTICIPATE RELENTLESSLY

"We must not allow our rulers to load us with perpetual debt.

We must make our election between economy and liberty or profusion and servitude.

If we run into such debt, as that we must be taxed in our meat and in our drink, in our necessities and our comforts, in our labors and our amusements, for our calling and our creeds...(we will) have no time to think, no means of calling our miss-managers to account but be glad to obtain subsistence by hiring ourselves to rivet their chains on the neck of our fellow sufferers. ...And this is the tendency of all human governments.

A departure from principle in one instance becomes a precedent...till the bulk of society is reduced to be mere automatons of misery. ...And the fore-horse of this frightful team is public debt. Taxation follows that, and in its train wretchedness and oppression."

—Thomas Jefferson

LINKS TO GOVERNMENT INFORMATION & INTERNET SITES

There are thousands of websites that provide information and networking to people desiring to take America back. I include a few here to get you started on the road to information and empowerment.

C-Span has extensive, vital government information on their website:

C-Span: http://www.c-span.org/
http://www.c-span.org/Resources/State-Local.aspx
http://www.c-span.org/Resources/Media-Organizations.aspx
http://www.c-span.org/Resources/White-House-Executive.aspx
http://www.c-span.org/Resources/Supreme-Court-Judiciary.aspx
http://www.c-span.org/Resources/Congress-Legislative.aspx
http://www.c-span.org/Topics/Politics.aspx

C-Span, cont'd: http:// www.capitolhearings.org/

From the Miller Center of Public Affairs, University of Virginia, a record of presidential speeches:
Presidential Speeches: http://millercenter.org/ scripps/archive/speeches/nixon/index

Barack Obama's Office of Public Liaison : http://www.whitehouse.gov/administration/ eop/opl/

US Senate: http://www.senate.gov/

US House of Representatives: http://www.house.gov/

House Committee on Financial Services: http://financialservices.house.gov/

National Archives: http://www.archives.gov/

Other Important Websites & Alternative News:

Track Actions of Congress: http://www.govtrack.us/about.xpd

Investigate Money in State Politics: http://followthemoney.org

Citizens for Legitimate Government: http://legitgov.org/

OpEdNews:http://www.opednews.com/
index.php

Sunshine Week:http://www.sunshineweek.org/

Campaign for Liberty:http://
www.campaignforliberty.com/index.php

**News and links to some state government
agencies and executive branches, USA Regional
News:**http://www.usa-regional.com/Index/
News_and_Media

Fillibuster Info: http://www.filibusted.us/

World Net Daily:http://www.wnd.com/

Campaign Contributions Tracker:
http://www.newsmeat.com/

Meetup Groups: http://firecongressmeetup.com

Alternative news:
http://www.globalresearch.ca/

The Bill of Rights Defense Committee:
http://www.bordc.org/

   __Visit the author's blog,__ **"Poor Naomi's
Almanac,"** for critical updates, to join with
others, and to keep abreast of our democratic
health, here:
         http://10com.wordpress.com/

AN ANCIENT TALE

There once was a youthful boy, very special was he, filled with wondrous possibility. He loved the land, the forest, the hills and valleys. One day, when he was taking his usual walk, he met up with a snake.

Imagine his great awe when the snake called up to him, and said (most naturally, which made it all the more interesting) "Boy! Hello there, Boy! Fine day for your fine two legs! —Wish I had legs. I'm so in need of a ride to the top of this hill. Will you carry me up with you?"

The boy broke into a sly grin. Surely, he had found a most valuable thing...a talking snake. Still, he had a natural caution, borne of instinct, as he had some knowledge of the dangers of the wild. He was no snake's fool.

"Ha! Surely you jest! I'm not going to carry you! You are a snake, and you will bite me!"

They regarded one another in a brief, suspended silence. Then, the snake appeared to droop in disappointment. "I can't believe how disillusioned you are. I am a talking snake, and surely you must note my greatness and my immense intelligence. I am a reasonable being, and I assure you, I just need a ride to the top of the hill. I won't bite you for helping me!"

The boy jabbed his sneaker into the dirt, taken in by the snake's most astonishing talent and his assuring words. Somehow, this sort of thing didn't feel quite right, but the snake was convincing and he really didn't want to be unkind. He was a very polite boy.

"Well, then, if you promise not to bite me, I'll carry you to the top." Gathering up his willing rider, the boy began his steep ascent. All the way, the snake talked non-stop and kept the boy very entertained.

On arriving at the peak of the hill, the boy stretched out his arms to let the snake to the ground, when swift and vicious the snake sank his fangs deep into the boy's hand. "OWWWWWW!" the boy cried. "You said you would not bite me if I carried you here!!"

As the snake slithered away, he answered the
boy with a new and totally indifferent tone. "I
am a snake. What did you expect?"

———————————

Like the boy in this old wisdom tale, we often fail
to understand the essential nature of people
and things. When it comes to the discernment
of another being's intentions, we can
innocently fail to take into consideration their
true natures...until we are bitten and finally
made wise.

Politicians make promises, they engage us with
clever words. — But their actions are often
opposite of what they promised, their
behavior after election is often not consistent
with the personality who campaigned for the
vote...for the ride to the top of the hill.

Those who are politically driven are most often
charming by nature and they understand how
to ply others to gain support, but all-too-
often, they are not as focused on the good of
their constituents as they promised.

Let us learn about the essential natures of the people that we choose to represent us, and not be sidetracked by great oration or the art of pretense. Most of all, once bitten by actions that belie their words, may we determine we shall not continue to carry the snake-who-is-just-being-himself, in order to be bitten again.

Let us be wiser than the cunning snake or the naïve boy. Much wiser.

ABOUT THE AUTHOR

"Naomi Silverthorn" is a satirical nom de plume of author Diana Lewis. Born to an Illinois farm family, their lives embodied the day-to-day challenges and struggles of average Americans. She was taught the sturdy, self-reliant mindset her family inherited from colonial ancestors dating back to the 1600s when the shores of New York and New Jersey were first colonized.

Having lost both parents to illness at an early age, she began a lifelong quest to be of service to others who suffered, the motivation she needed to found and operate a health care service, and later, to create a small, socially conscious publishing company. Over many years, she witnessed and shared in other people's personal struggles and listened carefully to the critiques of government from average Americans like herself, whose lives, liberty, and legacy she champions in this book.

Order Form

The Ten Commandments of Political Office
by Naomi Silverthorn   **$14.95 ea. U.S.**

Use this original form and take a discount:*

$4.00 discount on purchases of $44.85-$59.80 (3-4 books)
$8.00 discount on purchases of $74.75-$134.55 (5-9 books)
$15.00 discount on purchases of $149.50-$284.05 (10-19 books)
$45.00 discount on purchases of 20 books or more
Photocopies cannot be accepted. One discount form per person & household.

Shipping/Handling $3.50 first book per shipping address.
Add $2.00 per additional book to same shipping address.
KY residents add 6% sales tax

Checks Payable to: *TVD & Consulting*   Total Enclosed:$_____

☐ VISA

☐ MASTERCARD   **Signature** for credit card purchase:

Card Number in Digits: X_____

Exp. Date

Cardholder Name:_____   Mo.   Year

SHIPPING ADDRESS

Name:_____Address:_____City:_____

_____State:_____Zip:____Daytime Phone:_____

CARDHOLDER'S ADDRESS (If different from shipping address)

Name:_____Address:_____City:_____

_____State:_____Zip:____Daytime Phone:_____

We ship USPS or UPS Ground, depending on order size and weight.

TVD & Consulting
PMB 333, 1811 N. Dixie, Ste.104
Elizabethtown, KY 42701.
ORDER BY PHONE: 270-766-1380